¡GASPAR!

A Spanish Poet / Priest in the Nicaraguan Revolution

Bilingual Press / Editorial Bilingüe

General Editor
  Gary D. Keller

Managing Editor
  Karen S. Van Hooft

Associate Editors
  Ann Waggoner Aken
  Theresa Hannon

Assistant Editor
  Linda St. George Thurston

Editorial Consultants
  Barbara Firoozye
  David Koen
  Janet Woolum

Editorial Board
  Juan Goytisolo
  Francisco Jiménez
  Eduardo Rivera
  Severo Sarduy
  Mario Vargas Llosa

Address:
Bilingual Press
Hispanic Research Center
Arizona State University
Box 872702
Tempe, Arizona 85287-2702
(602) 965-3867

¡GASPAR!

A Spanish Poet / Priest
in the Nicaraguan Revolution

David Gullette

Bilingual Press / Editorial Bilingüe

Tempe, Arizona

Acknowledgments

Major new marketing initiatives have been made possible by the Lila Wallace-Reader's Digest Literary Publishers Marketing Development Program, funded through a grant to the Council of Literary Magazines and Presses.

Some of these poems appeared in *Gaspar vive* (1981), a privately published biography by Padre Manuel Rodríguez García, and in *Cantos de amor y guerra* (1979), published by the Nicaraguan Ministry of Culture and selected and introduced by Ernesto Cardenal.

Cover designer Lynn Nees, Bidlack Creative Services

© 1994 by Bilingual Press/Editorial Bilingüe

ISBN 0-927534-37-1

Library of Congress Cataloging-in-Publication Data
        Gaspar! : a Spanish poet/priest in the Nicaraguan Revolution / David Gullette.
            p. cm.
        ISBN 0-927534-37-1 : $13.00
            1. García Laviana, Gaspar, 1941-1978. 2. Nicaragua—Politics and government—1937-1979. 3. Frente Sandinista de Liberación Nacional. 4. Catholic Church—Nicaragua—Clergy—Biography. 5. Poets, Spanish—20th century—Biography. I. García Laviana, Gaspar, 1941-1978. Poems. Selections. English & Spanish. 1994. II. Title.
        PQ6657.A6695Z67   1994
        861—dc20   93-41109
                                                                        CIP

PRINTED IN THE UNITED STATES OF AMERICA

Dedico este libro al pueblo sanjuaneño
de todo corazón.

Foreword

On December 11, 1978 a Spanish priest named Gaspar García Laviana died near Orosí, Nicaragua, when he was raked by machine gun fire during a skirmish with Anastasio Somoza's National Guard. Beneath his red and black bandana was a cross, and in his hands was an automatic rifle.

How this thoughtful, rash, reserved, flamboyant, secretive, gregarious, much loved and loving man, so feared and hated by Somoza, came to be lying dead in the mud that rainy morning not far from the Costa Rican border is the subject of this book.

Gaspar was above all a priest, one who loved his people with an uncompromising intensity; one whose attempts as a parish priest to better through peaceful means the lives of the Nicaraguan poor had been baffled at every step; one who felt that embracing armed struggle against a tyrant was not only justified, but in his case, unavoidable; one whose publicly stated rationale for taking up arms gave the Sandinistas fighting against Somoza a broad ethical, even spiritual, legitimacy they had previously lacked in Christian Nicaragua.

But few of his parishioners knew that he was also a poet, and had quietly chronicled the progress of his emotional, political, and moral development in passionate but tightly disciplined verses.

In these pages we will learn how a priest arrived at the decision to take up arms. But we will also hear a masterful poet speak to us directly about the beauty and squalor of his adopted homeland, about his love for the poor, about his anger against official indifference and brutality, about his hopes for the future, and about the death he saw clearly waiting for him just up the path at the top of the hill.

This book has three main sources: a privately published biography by Padre Manuel Rodríguez García (like Gaspar, a Missionary of the Sacred Heart) titled *Gaspar vive* (1981); Gaspar's poems, as printed in Padre Manuel's book, as published in *Cantos de amor y guerra* (1979), selected and introduced by Ernesto Cardenal, as well as a handful of previously unpublished poems Padre Manuel has made available to me; and my own interviews with citizens of San Juan del Sur, Nicaragua, who knew and loved Gaspar as though he were a son and brother and not merely a parish priest.

A few words about the sources.

Gaspar vive presents certain problems for a scholar trained to care about careful attribution. Padre Manuel has strung together multiple eyewitness testimonies in free-flowing chapters that begin with the names of six or eight or ten informants, but seldom with any indication in the text of who has said what. Often the informants are identified only by first name. Often they contradict one another. The book is thus a communal biography of one man, with each informant, as Padre Manuel says, "carrying his or her grain of sand" to the composite whole. And as when many hands pull a rope at once, it's impossible to specify individual contributions.

But as I found when talking with sanjuaneños about Gaspar, even the most painstakingly objective researcher could not hope to arrive at fixed and final truths, especially about a man who excited such deep and often ambivalent emotions. One person showed me the boots he died in; another (later) said they couldn't be Gaspar's boots, his feet were much bigger; a third said the National Guard stole his boots; a fourth said they're buried under the Gaspar monument in the San Juan churchyard; a fifth said, no, he's buried in the churchyard in Tola (his other parish) wearing the very boots he died in. It is not that Nicaragua defies truth-telling; it is that Nicaraguan truth tends to be multiple, a fabric of crossed, tangled, conflicting threads that somehow end up suggesting a coherent design. As Eduardo Galeano says somewhere, the only trustworthy accounts of reality are those riddled with contradictions. In this sense, *Gaspar vive* is a quintessential Nicaraguan book.

The poems present their own set of difficulties. Ernesto Cardenal printed a collection of them, with titles, in *Cantos de amor y guerra* in

1979, the year of the Triumph. Padre Manuel reprinted some of the same poems, and many others not in *Cantos*, none with titles, in *Gaspar vive*. When I asked in San Juan about the original manuscripts of the poems, I was told (by one informant) that different people in the area had had originals of the poems in the late 1970s, but had burned them, fearing the consequences if Somoza's National Guard should find them in possession of poems written by "the Communist priest." But before being burnt, the poems were copied—either typed or written in longhand. My informant could not explain why copies would be less incriminating than originals, since presumably none bore the author's name. In any case, I was assured that the poems were carefully, faithfully copied. It was not clear which poems had undergone this Phoenix-like transformation. If this were a scholarly edition of Gaspar's poems—which some day we deserve to see—these textual uncertainties would be a cause for consternation. But this book is instead an introduction to his life and his writing for English-speaking readers, and I have had no choice but to trust the authenticity of the poems' texts as they have come down to us from Cardenal and Rodríguez. The poems themselves vary radically in length and degree of completeness. Some are formal and fully-wrought; others are mere unrevised fragments scribbled down in odd hours. As Ernesto Cardenal wrote to me recently, "Gaspar was not a professional poet. He was perhaps something more important than that."

The choice to counterpoint the biographical and historical narrative with some of Gaspar's poems is meant to suggest the parallels between his private mind and his public acts. To print the poems separately in an appendix would be to imply a disjunction between the poet, the priest, and the revolutionary. There was no such disjunction. I have presented the poems in bilingual format for the sake of those who realize that translation, far from being a mirror of the original, is merely another form of personally slanted "Nicaraguan truth."

Many residents of San Juan del Sur shared with me their memories of Gaspar. Most useful were the contributions of José Raúl Muñiz, Elena Valle Calderón, Carlos Guzmán, Teresa Guzmán, Emilio Gonzales ("Pájaro Loco," for many years Gaspar's lay assistant and companion on excursions to the backwoods), Catalina Navarro ("Catucha," Gaspar's cook and housekeeper), Padre Ramón Pardina, M.S.C., the former parish priest in San Juan del Sur, and Esperanza Rodríguez Calderón, who first introduced me to Gaspar's poetry. In Boston, the comments of Melissa Chinchillo,

Carol Sánchez Costello, and Pamela Bromberg have been particularly useful.

Above all, the encouragement and assistance of Padre Manuel Rodríguez García have been deeply heartening.

A final note about some frequently repeated Spanish terms. *Campesino* is usually translated as "peasant," a word with a slightly medieval sound in English. It means literally someone who works in the *campo* or countryside. Before the revolution, most campesinos lived lives much like those of sharecroppers in the American South, with all the poverty and exploitation and hopelessness that term connotes. That's the connotation to give Gaspar's use of the term. *Compañero* is sometimes translated as "comrade," a word with a slightly East Bloc sound in American English. In Central America, it traditionally has the neutral sense of friend, neighbor, coworker, or buddy, although in the last 20 years it has taken on a politicized (left-wing) connotation, especially in the Nicaraguan contraction *compa*. *Guerrilla* in Spanish is guerrilla warfare, not the person who fights that kind of war; the warrior we wrongly call "guerrilla" in English is called *guerrillero* in Spanish. Augusto César *Sandino* led the fight against the occupying U.S. Marines in the late 1920s and early 1930s; the Sandinista Front for National Liberation (FSLN) was founded in 1962 and modelled on Sandino's ideas. It is sometimes known in Nicaragua merely as *el Frente*. Its motto is "Patria libre o morir" (Free Fatherland or Death). Anastasio *Somoza*, Sr. was put in power by the U.S. Marines; he had Sandino murdered in 1934. His son Anastasio Somoza Debayle ("Tacho") was overthrown by the Sandinista-led revolution in 1979. *Somocismo* refers to the autocratic, repressive, predatory style of government and political life Nicaragua suffered under Tacho. Tacho's personal army was the *Guardia Nacional*, sometimes abbreviated as GN. The word *guardia* can also refer to a member of the Guardia Nacional.

A grant from The Simmons College Fund for Research made this book possible.

¡GASPAR!

A Spanish Poet / Priest in the Nicaraguan Revolution

✧ ✧ ✧ **1**

*One of the family photos shows a serene, handsome young priest
standing between his obviously proud mother and father. The year is
1966. He has the dark brows of his father, an Asturian miner, but
it is his mother's broad, almost playful smile we see in most of the
handful of photos that have come down to us: Gaspar in his
soutane surrounded by his brother Silverio and other friends; Gaspar
cutting the six-tiered cake at his ordination; Gaspar giving Holy
Communion to his kneeling parents; Gaspar blessing his flock in a
working-class barrio of Madrid; Gaspar saying goodbye to Archbishop
Morcillo of Madrid as the latter enters his limousine; and years later,
Gaspar in black beret, sleeves of his khaki shirt rolled up, standing in
front of the FSLN flag somewhere in Nicaragua, his rifle in his
hands. He wears the same smile: energetic, a bit mischievous,
determined–the smile of the happy warrior.*

In 1952, at the age of 11, the Asturian miner's son Gaspar García Laviana
was accepted into the Pequeña Obra del Sagrado Corazón, a school oper-
ated in Valladolid by the Missionaries of the Sacred Heart, an order
committed, long before Vatican II, to a preferential option for the poor.
Here the intense young man heard stories of the heroic sacrifices made by
missionaries of the order, struggling to better the lives of the downtrodden
in far away places with exotic names. He no doubt imagined himself, too,

engaged in titanic struggles against evil for the sake of the marginalized and forgotten children of God.

When the time came for further study, the new member of the Congregation of Missionaries of the Sacred Heart, just 18, made the journey to Logroño to attend the order's advanced college, the Escolasticado. There he distinguished himself as an actor and athlete. The discipline of the college was severe, but Gaspar managed to exhibit a wild streak, sneaking off occasionally on forbidden visits to the city.

It was in Logroño that Gaspar cemented his friendship with Pedro Regalado, a novice of about his age, with the same passion for social justice, although without Gaspar's impulsive rebellious streak. On one occasion Gaspar convinced Regalado to slip away with him from a retreat in the mountains to see a bullfight in the town of Estella. "We were," says Regalado, "like kids with new shoes. We laughed at anything and everything. Everything was new for us. It was our first 'disobedience.'" After the bullfight Gaspar suggested they make their way over the mountains to the dazzling international beach resort of San Sebastián. But at the end of the day they found themselves stuck there on the coast after the last bus back to Logroño had left. Whatever happened, they knew they had to be back at the Escolasticado in time for morning mass. They finally managed to catch a night train that brought them into Logroño at the crack of dawn. The authorities had been terribly worried; now they were furious. The boys were soundly rebuked. Recalling the escapade later, Gaspar would say: "Our suffering was greater than the fun we had."

But it was in social action that the two novices discovered their true callings. Working closely with young people in their catechism classes in poorer barrios, Gaspar and Regalado found themselves appalled by the living conditions of these former country folk who had flooded into the cities looking for work. Despite being assured by those with more experience that such a thing would be impossible, Gaspar formed a cooperative to build low-cost housing. Bureaucratic obstacles and the defeatism of the poor filled him with a sort of divine rage. Nothing was impossible! He bulled ahead; failure was not in his lexicon. And yet when setbacks occurred, he occasionally became depressed and withdrawn. Young people especially were drawn to him, ready to follow his lead. By the time Gaspar and Regalado left the Escolasticado in 1966, the housing cooperative in Barrio La Estrella had 328 members. It is still functioning today.

After his ordination in 1966, Gaspar spent several years as a "sacerdote obrero," a worker priest, in the parish of San Federico just outside Madrid, ostensibly assisting Padre Arturo García, the parish priest. You'd be as likely to find Gaspar banging away with his hammer or pushing a plane in the carpenter's shop where he worked eight hours a day, or in the street buying ice cream for kids, or bicycling down back roads to visit the sick, as in the church itself.

But what was a priest doing working in a carpenter's shop? At first the other workers were suspicious: the priest already had a job, there must be some fishy reason for him to be hanging out in a workshop. What's the story? But bit by bit, Gaspar's energy, enthusiasm, and guileless nature won them over. "He may be a little crazy, but he does his work like anyone else."

Still, among certain priests he began to gain a reputation as a "snob" slumming among the poor, pretending to be proletarian, a superficial priest interested in showy "social action" projects and forgetting his links with God. Gaspar seemed not to care what they said; his conscience was clear. And yet a crisis was brewing in his soul. Padre Manuel recounts a story from this period:

"One afternoon he makes his way to the Provincial Headquarters of the order. He goes directly to the office of the Provincial Director. At first they chat about inconsequential matters. It seems a visit like any other. But Gaspar clearly needs to unburden himself. 'I know what many people are saying about me. That I don't pray. That if I go on as I do things will turn out badly for me. Some even think there's nothing of the priest in me. But let me tell you something. I've never needed to pray more than I do now. And I do pray, every day, many times a day. Because I need help now, lots of help. And it's clear that the help others can give me is minimal, almost nothing. And that's why I pray. And that's why I keep on doing what I'm doing. And that's why I see clearly that I'm on the right path. I'm aware of the hand of God.'

"And yet one night he returns home desperate. It's two in the morning. Padre Arturo is in bed. Gaspar needs to talk, to open up, so he wakes him: 'Arturo, I've convinced myself that my work at the shop can never be the same as that of any other worker. I spend hours and hours stripping and planing wood and I tend to forget my priesthood. Come with me. Let's pray together.'"

And so Gaspar knelt with Arturo and prayed for advice. It was 1968, a watershed year both in Europe and throughout the Americas, a year in which many men and women were undergoing social, moral, and political transformations, a year in which students took to the streets, traditional power structures were challenged, the year of the Medellin Conference which issued a call for priests to combat social oppression, a year in which the progressive wing of the Catholic Church grew every day more militant.

A few months later, the Missionaries of the Sacred Heart launched a call for volunteers: Central America was desperately in need of priests. Gaspar submitted his name. So did Regalado.

November 1970: Four Spanish Missionaries of The Sacred Heart of Jesus flew from Madrid to Mexico City on their way to assignments in Central America. Gaspar and Regalado had been assigned to Nicaragua, Padres Ramón P. (Pardina) and Ramón R. would work in Guatemala. One would think that after seeing the rural poverty in Asturias and urban poverty in Logroño and Madrid, no human misery could shock Gaspar. But Mexico City horrified him.

Padre Ramón Pardina is, in the late 1980s, the parish priest of San Juan del Sur, Nicaragua, Gaspar's old seat. We sit at a big table in the Casa Cural. Out in the street the cries of birds mingle with the sounds of a band as the people of San Juan carry a scarlet-robed statue of Christ through the streets of the town. Tonight, on the eve of Easter, Padre Ramón will light a fire on the pavement before the monument to Gaspar and, as the wind roars down from the hills, will bless the flames. He speaks in crisp, deliberate Spanish:

"The kind of education we had received in Spain, whether in the schools under the Franco dictatorship or in the seminaries of the Spanish church, was very traditional, very right-of-center. And we who had been educated in the seminary had very limited ideas of our missions: to baptize, to hear confession, to say mass, to marry people, to prepare them, that is, to go to heaven. The first real impact the Americas made on Gaspar was in Mexico City. . . .

"We flew to Mexico City from Madrid, slept there, and on the following day took the opportunity to see the city. We all had our eyes open, but it was Gaspar who was particularly struck to see the contrast between streets and houses, the buildings so . . . so luxurious, and at the same time, almost side by side, barrios, streets, and houses of extraordinary poverty.

". . . In Spain, in Madrid, there are rich sections and poor sections. But the contrast is not as marked as in Mexico. . . . We could tell, Gaspar was deeply moved."

Gaspar began to wonder, says Padre Ramón, if the traditional role of the priest would be sufficient to meet the needs of the poor. What kind of priest would the downtrodden of the New World require?

❖

Finally, Gaspar and Regalado arrived in San Juan del Sur, where they were met by a member of their order, Padre Pedro, who had been asked to remain until their arrival, after which he planned to return to his mission in Guatemala. After an exchange of greetings, Gaspar suddenly said, "We need you here in Nicaragua. Don't leave." Pedro decided to stay, and would later play a crucial role in the revolution.

Gaspar was supposed to be the priest for San Juan and Regalado for Tola, a smaller town about 20 miles away. But the two young priests made a solemn pact:

—They would never split up. They would both live in San Juan, and travel to Tola for priestly duties;

—If unforeseen circumstances should force them to work separately, they would make the decision based on what was best for the two of them as a unit, not for one or the other;

—They would work principally with and for the poor and oppressed;

—As long as the oppressed lived worse than the bishop and other priests, they would contribute no parish funds to the diocese in Granada;

—They would create a Parish Economic Committee which would administer all the funds of the parish; and

—Their own way of life would resemble as closely as possible the life of the people.

❖

San Juan del Sur is spread around a half-moon bay on the Pacific coast just north of the Nicaraguan-Costa Rican border. As in 1970 when Gaspar and Regalado arrived, the economic life of the town is based mainly on fishing, a sporadically lucrative and occasionally dangerous trade. Ferocious offshore winds frequently burst down from the hills, twist themselves into waterspouts that can capsize a small boat or drive one with engine trouble far out to sea. The fishermen, who from time to time double as stevedores at the port, tend to oscillate between boom and bust. When

7

money comes in, there are blind spending sprees and widespread drunkenness. When times are slack, families suffer. Most of the fish is shipped immediately to Granada or Managua. Housing is shabby and overcrowded, sanitation abysmal, although a municipal sewage system has begun to be laid down. In 1970, there was one private doctor, but his services were prohibitively expensive for most people. In the 1980s there was an excellent free health clinic. In the post-Sandinista '90s, activists struggle to keep pay-as-you-go health care within reach of the poor.

There are some elegant houses, but when Gaspar arrived they belonged to wealthy people from Managua, including the Somozas, who used them once or twice a year. In 1970, there were only a few schools and they were too costly for the average family. Very few people knew how to read. Children began work at the age of five or six. In the 1980s there were free schools for all children and adult education classes held in the schools at night. In the free market '90s, illiteracy is on the rise again, and students above fourth grade pay a fee to go to "public" schools.

Behind the first range of hills are valleys with good soil and available water. Before the revolution large private landholders controlled the land. The campesinos worked on these farms for subsistence-level wages or were allotted small plots for sharecropping, with the landholder taking the lion's share of the harvest. In the aldeas, or hamlets, of the parish— Delicias, Escameca, Escamequita, La Flor and Ostional to the south, and Nacoscolo and El Bastón to the north, along the abandoned railbed road known as La Chocolata, and in small settlements scattered through the hills in the direction of Lake Nicaragua to the east—life was even harder than in San Juan. The diet was scant rations of corn for tortillas, maybe a banana or plantain now and then, and rice and beans which, when mixed together, make the national staple *gallo pinto* ("painted rooster"). Fish seldom reached the backwoods. Now, as then, in April, toward the end of the dry season, when the land heats up and the poroporo trees blossom in a splash of yellow against the brown hills, a lucky campesino with a feisty dog is able to defy the Endangered Species law and scare up a few garrobo, an iguanalike lizard that makes an excellent cornmeal-thickened stew, *pebre de garrobo*. But for the most part the campesinos Gaspar encountered were malnourished, chronically sick, ignorant, exploited, and yet stubbornly fixed in their ways. It was this widespread unwillingness to entertain even the possibility of change, of communal action, of breaking out of an automatic fatalism inherited from their parents, that frustrated and saddened Gaspar most. One of his earliest poems puts it bluntly:

8

Tu peor mal, campesino
no es la falta de la tierra,
ni el hambre,
ni la enfermedad;
tu peor mal
está en no darte cuenta,
está en ti mismo.

Your worst problem, campesino
isn't the lack of land,
nor hunger,
nor sickness;
your worst problem
is not being aware:
it's inside you.

Tu peor traba, campesino
no es la opresión,
ni la Guardia,
ni los ricos;
tu peor traba
es la desunión,
está en ti mismo

Your greatest obstacle, campesino
isn't oppression,
nor the Guardia,
nor the rich;
your greatest obstacle
is your disunity,
it's inside you.

Gaspar began to settle into life in San Juan. He went out of his way to visit people in their homes, spending long hours chatting, visiting the sick, sharing meals, getting to know about the lives of his new parishioners. He charmed them with his tales of life at home in Spain, his mother's cooking, his siblings, his father's work as a miner. Sometimes he sang songs from Asturias. People passing by a house at night knew Gaspar was there by his hearty, infectious laughter. They'd never known such an informal, friendly priest. In fact, some wondered, how serious could he be, always laughing and slapping you on the back?

But he was also drinking in details: the skimpy meals, a child's lingering cough, a mother's threadbare skirt, dirty-faced kids playing in shabby yards where foul-smelling water trickled through pig feces, the bad teeth, the drunken fathers, the sounds of weeping at night, the sighs of resignation when trouble struck, the bent posture of people accustomed to defeat, the washed-out eyes.

La pobreza,
hambre vieja
de San Juan,
va grabando
la tristeza
en las caras
afiladas

Poverty,
age-old hunger
of San Juan,
carves
sadness
in the gaunt
faces

9

de los pobres	of the poor
que se van.	who come, then go.
Cabalgando	Mounted
en la nada	on the nothing
de los hombres	of people's lives
la pobreza	poverty
anda suelta	ranges free:
y no se va.	it always comes, it never goes.

The Casa Cural, or parsonage, in San Juan is a large, elegant house from the 1950s, with ample rooms, high ceilings, and a splendid walled garden. When he arrived, Gaspar was mortified that it was "all his." It was grander than any house he'd ever lived in, at a time in his life when he'd made a conscious decision to live as much as possible like the poor. So he tried opening the house up as a sort of community center, available to all, but this didn't solve the problem of campesinos who came in from the countryside to do marketing but had little time to receive religious instruction or other services. Often, by the time night fell, they had barely completed their tasks and were forced to make the long, difficult journey back to the aldeas in the dark. The Casa Cural wasn't really suitable for many overnight guests. So Gaspar decided to construct a "Casa Comunal" with dormitories, sanitary facilities, and meeting rooms for church organizations, such as the Delegates of the Word. He organized fiestas and bazaars to raise money for construction. Even only partly finished, the Casa Comunal became a home away from home for campesinos visiting town. Sometimes Gaspar stretched out on a cot next to the campesinos and passed the night with them, as he had begun to do when he visited them in the backwoods. But the contrast between his relative privilege and their poverty always gnawed at him.

En la paz de mi noche sin fronteras	In the peace of my limitless night
pensaba en la negra noche de los pobres;	I thought of the black night of the poor;
pensaba en la inacabable soledad del oprimido,	I thought of the endless solitude of the oppressed,
en la angustia del obrero cuando le dan el despedido.	of the anguish of the worker when he's fired,

Y pensaba en la quimera que es la dignidad del hombre.	and I thought of that fleeting illusion which is human dignity.
La dignidad del pobre es la miseria, el devorar en silencio el pan de la tristeza, el dormir su negra noche en el olvido, el vivir y morir sin hacer ruido. En la paz de mi noche verdadera sentí, pobre, que era mía tu pobreza.	Misery is the dignity of the poor, eating the bread of sadness in silence, sleeping their black nights in oblivion, living and dying without making a sound. In the peace of a true night I felt, poor brother, that your poverty was mine.

In his first year or so in San Juan del Sur, Gaspar embarked upon a series of well-intentioned campaigns to improve the life of the people. Almost all met with failure, to one degree or another. One of the first was an attack on the endemic drunkenness that plagued the town. Gaspar organized a "club" in the Casa Cural where in the afternoon and evening (prime hours for getting drunk) adults of drinking age could gather for discussion and debate or to play chess, dominos, cards, or Ping-Pong, accompanied by copious drafts of some nonalcoholic "refresco" of fruit juices. The club was a great success, at first. But soon attendance began to wane, and the shouts and laughter of the remaining core of regulars convinced most people that Padre Gaspar had opened a drinking club. Gaspar himself began to wonder if there weren't a little under-the-table pouring of rum going on. His occasionally explosive temper alienated many of the club's "members." At other times he took the trouble to bring drunks in off the street or from the church steps, strip them, put them in a cold shower until they sobered up a bit, get them dressed again, and then lead them home. And he began to wonder: Why did they feel they needed to drink? Why was rum so cheap and easily available? Did somocismo benefit from a drunk and, therefore, politically somnolent populace? What was it that might replace the hopelessness and poverty that drove so many to drink?

At least a drunk acknowledges his heartache. Could the same be said of Padre Gaspar?

11

Contaba un hombre en la calle	A man in the street told
las penas del corazón.	the sorrows of his heart.
El hombre estaba borracho.	The man was drunk.
Yo no.	Not I.
Nos explicó que sufría	He explained to us how he
por una traición de amor.	suffered
El hombre amaba a alguien.	a loved one's betrayal.
Yo no.	The man was in love with
	someone.
	Not I.
El hombre estaba borracho	The man was drunk
y contaba su amor.	and told of his love.
El borracho era sincero	The drunk was sincere.
Yo no.	Not I.

In an attempt to better the working conditions of the stevedores, Gaspar offered a three-day course of lectures on trade unionism. But scarcely had the lecture begun than an "expert" on trade unionism from Managua arrived (no one knew how he learned about the course). He recounted, in an impressive fashion, a series of "case histories" that illustrated how dangerous unions could be for the happiness and security of working people. He offered Gaspar and Regalado all the "help" they needed, including money. A discreet investigation discovered that he was a spy, under contract to the CIA. The priests politely declined the help. But the spark had gone out of the meetings, and the attempt to create a union or a worker's cooperative collapsed. And in some circles the word began to go around that San Juan had two "Communist priests."

In yet another campaign, Gaspar found funds for a dozen sewing machines and a teacher to show women how to sew their own clothes. But problems arose almost instantly. Suspicions and ill feelings prevailed. Which women would get to keep the machines in their homes? Who would get to use them first? Why should others have to wait? Gaspar urged the teacher to push ahead despite the bickering, but bit by bit interest in the sewing workshop evaporated.

A campaign against war toys also flopped, despite Gaspar's impassioned plea from the pulpit that such toys "teach our children how to kill their brothers." And a plan to create a food cooperative to reduce the cost of feeding families foundered on the sanjuaneños' ingrained mistrust of communal efforts.

What Gaspar didn't realize early on about these failures is what he slowly, painfully came to realize later: that liberal palliatives were useless against the old fatalistic Nicaraguan mindset encouraged by somocismo; that what was needed was not more band-aids, but a new kind of Nicaraguan; and that he, Padre Gaspar, was still an outsider—well intentioned, no doubt, but not someone who knew in his bones and blood what it meant to be poor in Nicaragua. Neither he nor the average Nicaraguan was ready for self-transformation. As he would later write:

Las semillas del secano	Seeds that need drying
parecen ideologías.	are like ideologies.
Ha de pasar el verano	The dry months have to come
para que sean recogidas.	and go
	before the crop can be gathered.
El tiempo es el hortelano	Time is the gardener
que trabaja la cosecha.	working toward harvest.
Todavía es muy temprano	But it's still too soon
y queda mucha maleza.	and there are too many weeds.

But if Gaspar could not reform all of San Juan overnight, at least he could make important changes in the life of the parish and how it was organized. Following the example of progressive Spanish priests in the 1960s, who sought greater popular participation in the concrete affairs of the church, Gaspar not only stopped remitting parish funds to the diocese (which would ordinarily pay his salary and provide funds earmarked for specific parish expenses), he also created a Parochial Commission of laymen who would decide how parish funds were spent. Gaspar would be paid by the commission, not by the bishop. The first commission looked like this:

President: Mercedes C. de Ruiz
Vice-President: Manuel A. García Novoa
Secretary: Olga Urcuyo
Vice-Secretary: Francisco J. García
Treasurer: Carlos Guzmán
Vice-Treasurer: Padre Pedro Regalado Diez

13

Warden: Manuel Antonio Valle
Members:
Evenor Estrada
José del Carmen Calderón
Francisco García Altamirano
Roberta Danglada
José Raúl Muñiz
Emilio Gonzales
Maruja de Calero

For most of these sanjuaneños, it was their first experience of democracy and communal responsibility. The commission not only paid the salaries of Gaspar and Regalado (a laughable 600 córdobas a month—but the priests insisted they wanted to live like the poor), it also decided how best to use the limited funds to meet the needs of the most desperate people in the parish. Those who could contribute most would do so; those who needed most, would receive.

It was during this period of the first Parochial Commission that Gaspar began to get his reputation as the "Penniless Priest." No sooner was his monthly salary paid than he would head for the aldeas of the back country, and return a few days later with his pockets empty. Catucha, his cook and housekeeper, complained that there wasn't enough to cover household expenses. Gaspar pretended that he was feeding his one vice, tobacco. In fact, most of the tobacco he'd bought, and all the rest of the money, had been distributed to the campesinos.

He also neglected his clothes. He wore the same pair of jeans and a cotton shirt day after day. "Sometimes," says Catucha, "someone would give him a nice pair of pants, or shoes, or a shirt, and I'd have to hide them, keep them in reserve, otherwise he'd just give them away to the first needy person he came across. He was like that. Owning clothes meant nothing to him. If he had his way, he'd be as naked as Adam."

Once, his colleague Padre Luis (who would become San Juan's priest after Gaspar's death) arrived for a visit, leaving his bag of clothes at the Casa Cural while he went to see old friends around town. Meanwhile Gaspar returned home, saw the clothes, assumed someone had given them to him, and promptly gave them away to two young campesinos who happened to be in town. When Luis came back to the Casa Cural and asked for his clothes, no one knew where they were. He grew angry and demanded they be found. Then Gaspar: "Oh, *those* clothes. I gave

14

them away. I thought . . ." And he began to laugh, so hard that finally Luis's anger dissolved and he too roared with laughter.

Gaspar was equally generous with money. If you mentioned a need, Gaspar's hand went into his pocket. He never made loans, only gifts. He wouldn't accept payment. Sometimes he gave you twice what you said you needed "just to be on the safe side."

During this time when work on the Casa Comunal had begun, Gaspar began to spend more and more time eating, sleeping, working, and talking with his poorest parishioners. He slowly moved away from theory toward practice, away from merely giving good advice toward being a living example of what he believed.

Rich tourists from Granada and Managua came to San Juan, some for extended stays. Gaspar hated the way their conspicuous wealth clashed with the poverty of San Juan and acted as a subtle rebuke against the poor. And yet some tourists had made a habit of contributing handsomely to the church.

One such woman, hearing of the Casa Comunal under construction, complained to the Parochial Commission that her money was meant for the needs of the church, not for housing a bunch of vagabonds. Word of her complaint reached Gaspar.

"Tell that woman not to give one more córdoba to the church. She doesn't know what the church is. The church is also the needy, the poor, those who lack education. They are her neighbors. We've got to love them as we love ourselves. No more money from her! It's . . . I mean, why should we accept her money if she doesn't know how to love her neighbor?"

There were also grumblings from Granada. The diocese was upset at San Juan's failure to remit parish funds. This only increased Gaspar's anger.

The poem is heavy-handed, but it makes its point:

También tú, Iglesia Secular,	You too, Worldly Church,
eres cliente de nuestro socialismo	could profit from our socialism
porque tienes que empezar a	because you need to start
practicar	practicing true Christianity.
el cristianismo.	

15

Cristo rechazó la riqueza,	Christ rejected wealth
pero tú buscas los ricos	but you seek out the rich
y tienes la pobreza	and think of poverty
como un mito.	as a myth.

Recuerda que Cristo vivió la	Remember: Christ lived the
igualdad	equality
que nosotros practicamos	that we practice
y tú siembras la desigualdad	while you sow inequality
en los cristianos.	among Christians.

The poetry. It's not clear exactly when Gaspar began to write poetry, but is was early in his Nicaraguan experience. Even as people were buzzing with news that they saw the priest in a swimsuit taking a youth group to the beach or saw him running to a meeting or speeding off to visit the sick in the hospital in Rivas, even in the midst of this frenetic activity centered on the needs of others, Gaspar made a point of breaking his busy schedule every three or four weeks to take a few days off for solitary meditation, prayer, and writing. Sometimes it was to a little farmhouse in the hills near San Juan; sometimes he spent time over at San Jorge on the shore of "the world's most beautiful lake."

Some of his early poems are examples of careful observation by a thoughtful mind that realizes how deceptive the surface of things can be.

Nube blanca	White cloud
navegaba	was sailing
muy nerviosa	uneasily
por el lago.	down the lake.

Eran garzas.	It was egrets.

En la orilla	At the edge
de mi lago	of my lake
el madero	the madero tree
cosechaba	was gathering
gasa blanca	white gauze
y algodones.	and cotton.

Eran garzas.	It was egrets.

La ribera	The shorefront
de mi lago	of my lake
vio un desfile:	saw a long procession:
Eran vacas	There were cows
enfiladas	single file
jalonadas	urged on
de vaqueros	by cowboys
rutilantes	all glistening
de blancura.	white.
Los vaqueros	The cowboys
eran garzas.	were egrets.

Or the poet's life parallels the life of nature without quite mixing with it:

Acostado en la tijera	Stretched out on the cot
golpeaba la pared	I drummed the wall
con yemas de mis dedos	with my fingertips
y mezclaba mi cerebro su sonido	and my mind mixed that sound
con el ruido de las yemas	with the noise of the clouds'
de los dedos de las nubes	fingertips beating and beating
en mi tejado de cinc.	on my old tin roof.

But more typically, descriptions of the natural world become humanized, even moralized, as though all of creation were dreaming of some heroic action, as in the poem about the zanate (boat-tailed grackle):

Jii jii, jii.	Hee! Hee! Hee!
El zanate frente al lago	The zanate confronting the lake
se mantiene cara al viento	keeps his face up into the wind
al plumaje alborotado	his plumage ruffled and whipped
y el sonoro pico abierto.	and his tuneful beak wide open.
Jii, jii, jii.	Hee! Hee! Hee!
Cuando azota la tormenta	When the storm comes flailing in
el zanate se la enfrenta.	the zanate holds his ground.
¡Silba el zanate más recio!	The zanate whistles more strongly!
Jii, jii, jii.	Hee! Hee! Hee!
Jii, jii, jii.	Hee! Hee! Hee!

There is also a vein of self-questioning, as in the poem quoted on pages 13-14 in which Gaspar wonders why a drunk in the street is more capable

17

of unreflecting love than he is, or the following fragment, which may or may not be aimed at himself:

El dolor ajeno	The pain of others
pasa por nosotros	goes by us
sin calarnos adentro.	without sinking in.

The urge to love, however, presses through the romanticized landscapes and nature studies, love for the people, but also an almost eroticized love for the Companion, the Friend:

Te recortaste de luz	You were outlined by light
en la noche de mi casa	that night in my house
y te apreté contra mí	and I pressed you against myself
como aprieta el mar a la playa.	as the sea presses against the
No sentí nada en la piel,	shore.
te sentí toda en el alma.	I felt nothing in the flesh,
	all I felt was you in my soul.

But what these short retreats could not do was insulate him from thoughts of his beloved campesinos, whose sufferings began to eat away at him like a chronic pain:

Me hieren	They wound me,
tus mortajas	your premature
prematuras	shrouds
de hambre	of patient
serena.	hunger.
Me hieren	They wound me,
tus huesos	your bones
entubados	enclosed
en pieles	in thirsty
sedientas.	flesh.
Me hieren	They wound me,
tus ojos	your downcast
humillados	eyes
hendiendo	cleaving
la tierra.	the earth.
Me hieren	They wound me,
tu duro trabajo	your hard work

y tus malas	and your bad
cosechas.	harvests.
Me hieren	They wound me,
tu ignorancia	your ignorance
y tu eterna	and your eternal
tristeza.	sadness.
Me hieren	They wound me,
tus plantas	your bare
desnudas	feet
cuando pisan	when they tread
las piedras.	on rocks.
Todo tuyo	Everything about you
me hiere,	wounds me,
campesino,	campesino,
pero me hiere	but what wounds me
sobre todo	most of all
tu impotencia.	is your powerlessness.

And yet how do you empower those whose lives for generations have been a long series of defeats, who think of power as something only the rich can afford? What is the logical conclusion to be drawn from this wound the poet feels? Is compassion alone sufficient?

❖ ❖ ❖ 2

Gaspar's little white Renault had made the trip between San Juan and the hospital in Rivas so many times that people said the car could do it blind, with no driver. It was because more than anyone else Gaspar kept his finger on the pulse of San Juan and the outlying aldeas; he knew who was sick and people knew how to send messages through the grapevine: "Whoever sees Padre Gaspar next, be sure to tell him to check Gloria Granja. She's feeling pretty bad. He may have to take her to Rivas."

Sometimes someone would knock on the door of the Casa Cural in the middle of the night. A campesino might have walked in over the hills with news of a crisis. Five minutes later the old Renault would be roaring through the streets of San Juan.

One night Gaspar had returned from an exhausting circuit of visits through the back country. He was hot, sweaty, and muddy. He had barely collapsed in a hammock on the porch when word arrived that an old man up in the hills was gravely ill with tetanus. Without changing, he hopped in the car and headed out over muddy roads that made the wheels slip and spin. When he arrived, it was clear the old man had only a few hours to live if he didn't get to a doctor. The family wrapped him in a blanket, lifted him into the car, and Gaspar sped toward Rivas, one hand on the wheel and the other around the old man's shoulder. He wiped the man's brow, sang to him, offered encouragement: "Hang on, viejo, we'll make it." But by the time they arrived in Rivas the old man had died.

21

Gaspar was in a grieving rage. "Too late, we're too late! Once again! Always late!"

One of his few friends on the hospital staff (many were somocistas, and writhed when Gaspar periodically assailed the health care system), Dr. Cañizales, tried to calm him. "It couldn't be helped, Padre." Gaspar exploded. "Couldn't be helped? Of course it could be helped! How can this so-called government let people live like this? Just because they live up in the hills, does that mean they have to die like rats? Aren't they human beings like you and me? Why don't they have medicine, doctors, teachers? Can you tell me that? Why can't they read or write? Why are they left to rot?"

He launched into a noisy tirade about shortages of medicines, black market pharmaceuticals, and the absence of doctors in the aldeas. "And who allows this to happen? You know perfectly well who! This is not a country, it's a slave state! A government of hustlers filling their pockets at the people's expense!"

His eyes were bright, sweat poured off him, he was trembling. Dr. Cañizales got him away from the crowd of doctors and nurses who had gathered and out to his car in the parking lot.

"Are you alright, Padre?

Gaspar didn't answer. His knuckles were white on the steering wheel. He pulled out of the lot, slower this time.

By morning, Gaspar had a burning fever and the trembling was worse. He had typhoid. Fortunately, a sanjuaneña named Chapita, whom he called his "private nurse," found the proper injection, and Gaspar survived. But he didn't forget.

Se moría José Pérez	José Pérez was dying
vestido de hambre diaria.	dressed in his usual hunger.
El miraba a los ojos	He looked into my eyes
y yo miraba el alma,	and I looked into his soul,
yo le hablaba en el oído	I spoke into his ears
y él me gritaba al alma,	and he shouted out to my soul,
él me cogía la mano	he took me by the hand,
y yo le entregaba el alma.	I held out to him my soul.
Se moría José Pérez	José Pérez was dying
vestido de hambre diaria.	dressed in his usual hunger.

A él le dolía el cuerpo	For him, his body was aching
a mí me dolía el alma,	for me, it was my soul,
a mí se me iba el llanto	out went my cry
a él se le iba el alma,	up went his soul,
a él le moría el cuerpo	for him his body was dying
a mí me moría el alma.	for me, it was my soul.
Cuando murió José Pérez	When José Pérez died
el hambre fue su mortaja.	hunger was his shroud.

❖

"I'm a milk addict, a real milkaholic. I'll never die as long as I have a glass of milk to lift to my lips." It became a sort of running joke in the parish, and Catucha always had milk waiting for Gaspar whenever he wanted it. On his visits to the aldeas, he would tell the campesinos about the milk of his childhood: "I sometimes think I was raised on nothing but milk. . . . The milk in Asturias is the best in the world. Sometimes when I was growing up we made a meal of milk and nothing else. It was so good when my mother served it!" As a result, the campesinos would offer Gaspar milk whenever they could.

But he soon realized that his glass of milk was a special privilege, like the eggs or occasional chicken he was served on his pastoral visits. Once, he and his driver for the day, Pedro Isidro, were offered a couple of fried eggs while the children of the house were spooning up their simple meal of beans.

"Why aren't the kids eating what we're eating?" Gaspar asked the woman.

"It's because there isn't enough, Padrecito."

"Well, give our food to the children, then. We're big and we can look out for ourselves. They need good food much more than we do." And then more angrily: "Let's get this straight: I'm never coming to bring you or anyone else in this village the word of God if you don't treat me just like anyone else. Understood?"

He put his eggs on the children's plates, taking some of their beans for himself. Despite his hunger, Pedro had no choice but to follow suit.

After this Gaspar never accepted milk or other special food from the poor. Maybe this example would convince them more than stern lectures.

The same problem arose when the poor tried to pay him for religious services rendered, just as they used to do in the old days with the occasional priest who passed through dispensing ceremonies. Gaspar: "This is impossible! I don't want your money. Go buy something to eat and leave me alone!"

To pay him when they couldn't afford to may have struck them as a way to "honor" him (or maybe propitiate a capricious God), but what it really did was to set him apart from them—alienation through elevation. Why couldn't they see the necessity of simple brotherhood and equality between a priest and the people? Why did he always have to be doing their thinking for them?

Quisiera que tu carreta	I wish your oxcart would
transportara mis ideas a tu casa	bring my ideas to your house
como el maíz o el trigo	like maize or wheat
y que las fueras desgranando	and that you'd take off
una a una	the kernels one by one
o que las majaras	or that you'd thresh them
como el arroz.	together like rice,
Pero que fueran tuyas	but that the ideas were yours,
como las cosechas.	just like the harvests.

❖

Gaspar came to realize that despite his prodigious energy and commitment, he couldn't singlehandedly serve all the people in the extended San Juan parish. He needed help, especially when it came to raising the consciousness of the campesinos and seeing to it that small victories were not erased by reversion to the old defeatist habits.

Following the example set by the Equipos de Pastoral Rural (Rural Pastoral Outreach Teams) that had been functioning here and there in Nicaragua for more than 15 years, Gaspar decided to accelerate the training of Delegates of the Word, laymen who would be prepared for work in urban barrios and rural communities on everything from health and education to discussions of the gospel. The stress on improving living conditions as a prerequisite for creating true piety became a cornerstone to Gaspar's thinking: "First we have to make complete human beings, then we can made good Christians."

Gaspar was responding to the main tenets of Liberation Theology as it had unfolded since Vatican II and the Medellín Conference: the material life of the poor is inseparable from their spiritual life; the poor must be taught to understand the nature of their existence and not think of all parts of it as unchangeable; the oppressed must not merely be recipients of priestly ministrations, but must learn how to become responsible leaders and teachers themselves; God loves the poor, not poverty; communal social action, even the challenging of entrenched power structures, is not incompatible with religious commitment. The key term in this movement was "concientización"—giving the oppressed the gift of *awareness*, a consciousness of why their lives are the way they are, and what must be done to change them.

His work with the Pastoral Rural and CEPA (Centro de Educación y Promoción Agraria), the blanket organization that linked its practitioners together, put Gaspar in touch with some of the most progressive figures in Nicaraguan Catholicism, many of whom would later be persecuted, imprisoned, or deported by Somoza.

The reaction of the established Church to the Pastoral Rural movement was predictable, as Padre Manuel relates:

"The Church hierarchy does not look favorably on these highly committed activities. It hears voices accusing the Pastoral Rural Outreach Teams of being 'Marxist troublemakers.' The campesinos are beginning to open their eyes, to understand their dignity as people, and this is a threat to the small Nicaraguan upper-class, afraid of losing its privileges. All this talk of greater social justice, of a more equitable sharing of land, of equality in all aspects of social life, sounds to their ears like dangerous philosophies imported from the Old World. Nothing good can come of changing the status quo. And so the Church hierarchy, under the influence of this view, decides to act. One of the bishops—Monsignor Vega, Bishop of Juigalpa—is delegated to put himself in direct contact with the Pastoral Rural priests and report on their activities. Monsignor Vega, with all the power invested in him as the representative of the chief religious organization of the nation, begins to attend the meetings held in various locations. But from the start the priests realize that he's 'watering outside the flowerpot.' The meetings turn into magisterial lessons about Marxism—its errors and evils, the Church's strict prohibition against accepting its tenets, the social and religious disaster that its transplantation into Nicaragua would entail. Such is his obsession over this 'fact,' that he never understands the actual field of endeavor nor the underlying intention of the Pastoral Rural Outreach Teams. On one occasion, at Tola, his words serve only to undermine the meeting and create an atmosphere of hostility toward a Church hierarchy which, fearful of any change that might undercut its own privileges and benefits, prefers to let things remain as they are, with all the ongoing injustice that implies.

"One of the key moments in Gaspar's life, and one that explains in a nutshell his later actions, was a meeting in Juigalpa. Monsignor Vega was, of course, present. The meeting unfolded like so many others: more lessons on the evils of Marxism. But other themes were also raised, among them, the necessity of helping the campesinos learn to understand their place in the social scheme. Monsignor Vega began to speak about the evils of this sort of education, which could be ill-focussed and misused. Infuriated, Gaspar accused the bishop of not understanding the Gospels: 'The poor are getting the Word of God, because they're entitled to it; the Good News is for everyone.'"

Gaspar's anger against the traditional Church's self-serving complacency grew stronger every day. Sacred rituals became meaningless when God's children were subjected to deprivations and suffering which a caring, activist Church could alleviate.

Las angustias	The anguish
de mi alma	of my soul
no las calma	is not calmed
el rosario	by the rosary
ni la misa	nor the mass
ni el brevario.	nor the breviary.
Mis angustias	My anguish
las mitigan	is soothed
las escuelas	by schools
en los valles	in the valleys,
el bienestar	by the campesino's
campesino	well-being,
la libertad	by freedom
en las calles	in the streets
y la paz	and peace
en los caminos.	on the roads.

❖

On Christmas Eve of 1972, a major earthquake destroyed most of Managua, killing thousands, and leaving tens of thousands homeless.

Gaspar and Regalado rushed to Managua to help in the immediate rescue efforts, but it soon became clear that many victims would need to be moved away from the chaos and rubble of the capital. The priests decided to suspend other projects in San Juan and Tola to devote all the resources of the two parishes to earthquake relief, as in fact many communities in the Department of Rivas had begun to do.

Within the first few weeks, Gaspar had arranged to bring more than 6,000 earthquake victims to Rivas, after which they would be placed in various locations around the Department. In San Juan, people worked day and night to build temporary housing, set up kitchens, and collect food and clothing. The population of the town doubled overnight.

Gaspar worked feverishly, with almost no sleep. He heard that there were hundreds of orphans in Managua; he formed a committee in the Rivas area that arranged for temporary homes for 200 of them. But when he went to Managua to get the kids, he was told they'd been "sent abroad" by the Guardia. Sent abroad? Where? No one seemed to know. By whose authority? No one seemed to know. Gaspar lodged a formal protest. In vain.

There didn't seem to be enough emergency food, clothing, and medicine in the Rivas area, despite large quantities of international aid that were supposed to have been sent down. When he asked around, Gaspar discovered that the local Guardia commander had stockpiled 60 percent of it, so he could sell it later. He went to Managua and demanded an investigation. One of Somoza's sons, Julio Somoza Portocarrero, went to San Juan to direct the inquiry. As a result, the civilian head of the Rivas area relief committee was fired, but the Guardia remained untouched. Gaspar was livid, but there was no time for complaints. There was too much to be done.

Shuttling back and forth between San Juan and Managua, Gaspar heard comparable stories of official corruption, diversion of international relief, and selling what should be given away. All indications pointed toward Tacho Somoza himself as the main beneficiary. Even some old somocistas were appalled by his rapacity. The earthquake and its sordid aftermath taught a series of vivid political lessons to the people of Nicaragua.

Exhausted after weeks of relief work, Gaspar and Regalado managed to wangle free passage back to Spain on a plane that had unloaded its shipment of emergency supplies. Their trip created a slight political problem with their Missionary Order because they'd been in Nicaragua only two

27

years, and the official time for their first visit home had not yet arrived. But the Provincial Head of the Congregation looked at the two sleepless, bleary-eyed priests and gave his permission.

Spain, however, was not Nicaragua. Gaspar tried to visit all the Congregation's locations throughout the country, feverishly setting forth what must have sounded to his listeners like a chaotic jumble of unworkable plans: he would round up teams of doctors and medical technicians and fly them to Nicaragua to aid the earthquake victims; he would appear on national TV to explain the tragic situation in Nicaragua; he would write a series of articles about "Nicaraguan Reality"; he would enter his poems in a national poetry contest and use the money for San Juan. . . . But the reception was cool to say the least. Who was this crazy young man? Why was he back from his assignment before the appointed time? Rules are meant to be respected, not broken. "What a lot of long faces we saw," Gaspar said later. "As though we'd committed a crime against the dignity of the Congregation."

Gaspar returned to Nicaragua empty handed, but not before he made a quick visit to Asturias to see his family and to drink long soothing glass after glass of cool white milk.

❖

Back in Nicaragua everyone was talking about the scandal of diverted international relief, about members of Somoza's inner circle with warehouses full of food while the people were dying of hunger, and about a black market in blood.

Gaspar fell into a foul humor, short-tempered, embittered by the invulnerability of somocismo, impatient when immediate solutions weren't found to difficult problems, angry at himself for what he saw as his laughably ineffectual efforts to change the world through religion, and angry at the campesinos for being so stubborn in their fatalism, so unwilling to think of a better future. At one point of extreme exasperation he cried, "Working with campesinos is like plowing the sea!"

Early 1973 was a low point in his Nicaraguan experience, but finally a major problem yielded to a carefully crafted solution and Gaspar regained his buoyant self-confidence.

The only health care available in San Juan was a small private clinic run by a Dr. Caldera. When Gaspar asked sick campesinos why they didn't see Dr. Caldera, they would answer, "We can't afford it, Padre." The typical charge for consultation and medicine ran between 200 and 600 córdobas, which was about the range of average monthly income for a campesino. Only if there were no other recourse in the case of a serious illness would they empty their savings and see Caldera. Sure, it was highway robbery, "but what can you do? That's the way things are, they can't be changed."

During his frequent visits to the hospital in Rivas (where the new hospital today bears Gaspar's name), Gaspar made friends with two dedicated, progressive doctors, Valdés and Cañizales. Gaspar decided to convert a small wooden house attached to the church into a health clinic and dispensary; he asked Drs. Valdés and Cañizales to volunteer to staff it twice a week. They agreed to serve without remuneration. As for medicine, they got some help from the Catholic relief agency Caritas Nacional, and Gaspar wrote impassioned pleas to drug companies in Germany and Spain who responded generously.

Meanwhile, Dr. Caldera was still in business and Gaspar learned that he had been charging his patients for medicine he'd received as free samples. For Gaspar, this was unforgivable. During the Good Friday Via Crucis procession through the streets of San Juan, Gaspar arranged to have the Fourteenth Station in front of Dr. Caldera's house. Gaspar gave a short, cutting sermon about those who betrayed Christ, about those who sold him for 30 pieces of silver, about those today who rob Christ's brothers and sisters, the poor, and about those whose professional thievery is backed up by an unjust government and the Guardia. . . .

His listeners were stunned by his frankness, but everyone knew what he meant. When the sermon ended, the crowd stood silent. Only Dr. Caldera could be heard behind the closed shutters of his house, shouting and cursing at "the Communists." But he didn't show his face.

One thing was true: he did have friends in the government, and they soon heard blistering accounts of the meddlesome priest of San Juan.

The little dispensary next to the church worked fine for a while; but frequently, emergencies required Drs. Valdés or Cañizales to be elsewhere during the days and hours it was supposed to be open. Besides, even when the doctors arrived on schedule, not all the campesinos who needed help could make it into town from their work in the fields. Madelina Flores, Gaspar's secretary and typist, offered a solution. She knew Dr. Francisco Vélez Chavarría up in Nandaime might be able to help. Gaspar visited Dr. Vélez, and they soon reached an agreement: Dr. Vélez promised to spend two complete days a week in San Juan—not the ideal solution from Gaspar's point of view, but better than nothing. In addition, the economic necessities of the dispensary were such that Dr. Vélez suggested they charge a nominal fee for services. Gaspar resisted, but finally saw that some money had to be generated. The compromise was that only those who could really afford it would pay. The fee was set at two córdobas a visit, including medicine, 1 percent of Dr. Caldera's lowest fee.

Sanjuaneños were dazzled: some weeks there were actually two doctors at the new dispensary!

After working in San Juan a while, Dr. Vélez decided to move there permanently, but he was going to need more income than the few córdobas the poor could give. Gaspar had a brilliant idea: he approached the five shrimping companies who worked out of San Juan—Nicamar, Galipaxa, Caribia, Plusmarplus, and Tonifish—and offered them what amounted to a prepaid medical plan. Depending on the number of workers, each firm would pay the dispensary a fixed monthly sum, and in turn Dr. Vélez would treat any of these workers free. The companies accepted, the dispensary thrived, and Dr. Vélez would remain even after the revolution triumphed, as director of the new, expanded Centro de Salud.

But despite a small success here or there, Gaspar felt burdened with a sense of incompleteness, a restless yearning for a less haphazard and isolated struggle. It was not clear to him how best to serve the people, and what was more, the people themselves seemed passive and unresponsive, no matter what he did. The irony of loving them openly whether they wanted it or not and the struggle for their liberation without their active participation preyed on his mind. At times he was filled with an apocalyptic rage that would almost prefer the death of his beloved campesinos to seeing them go on suffering.

Yo sé, yo sé	I know, I know
que estos versos	you won't read these verses,
no vas a leer,	campesino,
campesino,	because you don't know how to
porque no sabes	or because they won't let you.
o porque no te dejan.	
Pero no los escribo para ti	But I don't write them to you
por tu mano los escribo	because I write them for you
y en tu vida los leo,	it's with your hand I write them

para que tu vida y tu protesta	and in your life I read them
llenen el mundo	so that your life and your protest
como el aire,	will fill the world
para que el mundo respire	like air
campesino	so the world will breathe
y sienta tus calles	campesino
y vista tus harapas	and touch your calluses
y sienta tu hambre	and wear your rags
y sufra tu opresión	and feel your hunger
y sienta vergüenza	and suffer your oppression
de tenerte como hermano	and feel shame
y para que te traten como a tal	to have you as a brother
o que te maten	and either treat you as one
	or kill you.

Another poem is even more blunt and more extreme in its suggestion. The poet is the agonized spectator, the impotent outsider who wants at any cost relief from what he is forced to see.

Prefiero que mueras,	Better you should die,
hermano campesino,	brother campesino,
que verte así,	than that I should always see
tan destrozado,	you thus:
tan en agonía,	so shattered,
tan muriendo	in such agony,
sin morirte nunca.	always to be dying
	but never to die.

❖

It was not only the passivity of the campesinos that enraged him; it was also the indifference of the government authorities. Time after time he pleaded with bureaucrats for health care, teachers, and better nutrition for the people. He was brushed off, sometimes politely, sometimes unceremoniously.

Padre Ramón Pardina tells of one occasion when Gaspar took a group of campesinos to Managua and, despite being warned by the Guardia not to, they held a small demonstration outside the office of the Minister of Education, demanding schools and teachers to staff them. After a while the minister called Gaspar in, and with a great show of cordiality, welcomed him, put himself at Gaspar's service, wondered what the problem was, and said he was always ready to talk about education. . . .

"Fine," said Gaspar. "I came with some campesinos. They're the ones who want the schools. Let me call them in."

"I'm afraid that won't be possible," said the minister. "Just you, Padre Gaspar."

"If it's not all of us, it's none of us," said Gaspar.

The minister walked into his office and slammed the door.

But while the Somoza government was indifferent to the needs of the people, it began to take an increasing interest in the activist priests of San Juan and Tola. One night Gaspar and Regalado returned to the Casa Cural and when Gaspar went to his bedroom he discovered a half-naked woman standing in the doorway. He was struck dumb. Regalado arrived. The woman asked the priests if they wanted to party. Regalado joked nervously and told the woman she'd have to leave. But Gaspar was furious. He grabbed the woman by the arm and jerked her toward the front door. At the edge of the porch he gave her a kick in the rear and sent her sprawling into the yard. She shouted and groaned loudly, as though she were drunk. According to Regalado, Gaspar was trembling with anger.

Later they learned that the woman was sent by the Guardia. Apparently the idea was that a little sexual scandal might blunt the prestige of the young priests.

What complicated matters was that young women frequently found ways to be in the presence of the handsome, dynamic Gaspar. Often two or three girls would find some patently frivolous excuse to call at the Casa Cural, stay to chat, and be in no hurry to leave. Despite the coquetry, these visits were innocent enough; still, Gaspar tried his best to discourage them without leaving any hurt feelings.

But Emilio Gonzales tells of a subtler and more ominous attempt to compromise Gaspar:

A serious, attractive young woman arrives in San Juan and begins to work on projects for improving the life of the campesinos. Inevitably, she is thrown into contact with Gaspar. As it becomes clear their interests are similar, they begin to help each other. But one day she suggests to Gaspar that they take a day off and go to a nearby beach. He declines, she insists, and finally he agrees. Early in the morning on the day of the outing, Gaspar raps on the door of Emilio, who often accompanies him on his trips into the back country.

"Get up, Pájaro Loco. We're going to the beach."

"Today? I'm not sure I can make it today, Padre."

"Get dressed, brother. You're coming with me. I need you."

Emilio finally gets ready and Gaspar explains the situation. "Listen, whatever you do, Pájaro, don't leave me alone with her. Understand?" And so Emilio plays his part. He sits between Gaspar and the woman during the drive over the bumpy dirt roads, straddling the gearshift as best he can. On the beach, when she tries to get Gaspar to take a walk with her, Emilio says, "Wait for me. I love a good walk." He clings to them like a duenna. But the woman keeps trying to make her move. Finally, Gaspar turns to her, and with Emilio standing there, says, "Stop treating me the way a woman treats a man. Just stop."

The woman grows silent and then invents an excuse for them to return early to San Juan. The next day she leaves town and is never seen again.

These incidents with women and the unmistakable hand of the Guardia at work attempting to undermine him combined with his doubts about his efficacy in making a permanent difference in the lives of the poor. He became tense and preoccupied much of the time. He asked Dr. Valdés to give him tranquilizers, but they seemed to have no effect. He tried working harder, or conversely, organizing excursions with Emilio, José Raúl, Margarita Muñiz, and Regalado, or with the "scout troops" of youngsters he had organized. But a deep unrest lingered. At one point he wrote a Trappist monastery in Spain explaining his situation and asking what would be involved in his leaving Nicaragua to become a Trappist Brother, living a cloistered life of prayer and physical labor in a closed community. A month or so later the invitation from the Trappists arrived. When should they expect him?

Suddenly faced with an actual means of escape, he was forced to ask himself what he really wanted. He would stay. His destiny, however painful, would be among the poor of Nicaragua.

El amor es como el hambre,	Love is like hunger,
insaciable y soberana.	insatiable, all-powerful.
El amor es como un cáncer	Love is like a cancer
que va devorando el alma.	that eats up the soul.

❖

33

By the end of 1974, Gaspar's view of Nicaraguan social reality and of his relationship to the poor was ready to undergo a major shift. Padre Ramón has one analysis:

"He saw very clearly that poverty was the consequence of ignorance, and that ignorance was the consequence of not having schools, and so he took a great interest in seeing to it that in the outlying aldeas schools should be built. . . .

"But in many cases the campesinos had not the least interest in seeing their children learn how to read and write. Because of their ignorance and poverty, the parents would expect a child of eight to go to work for the family, to make a few centavos. This upset Gaspar terribly. But the more he thought about it, the more he came to realize bit by bit that the problem was not simply ignorance or a lack of medical attention, but that the problem was much deeper, that there was a system, a highly organized system that saw to it that there would always be a large supply of poor people and consequently a large supply of dirt cheap labor available.

"And making sure that there would always be poverty, always be ignorance, were a handful of families who were able to live not simply the lives of rich people, but lives of real luxury and wealth—frequent trips to Miami, clothes for the wife from Miami, perfume from Miami, and the children sent to the best universities in the United States, France, or Germany. And to maintain this life it was necessary that the great majority of the people should live in abject poverty. Gaspar understood that this system fully coincided with the capitalist system of North American imperialism, which required a base of many very poor countries to maintain one country in great riches.

"And yet here he was, working with campesinos trying to get them interested in education, not always successfully. And he had to ask himself: if we have so much trouble trying to change the way of life of a few dozen campesinos, how in the world are we going to change all of Nicaragua?

"And so he came to see that the institutions of government in Somoza's Nicaragua were all lies, a deception, a smokescreen, a trap. That the system itself was the enemy. And he began to wonder whether he wasn't in his own way serving that system with his reformist activities that did nothing to change the larger structure, becoming an advocate for campesinos instead of teaching them how to be advocates for themselves, teaching them how to demand for themselves what they wanted from the government."

❖

Coming to understand the systematic oppression of the people under somocismo and at the same time losing faith in short-term palliatives and his own desperate individual efforts, Gaspar began to seek broader, more highly organized forms of struggle. It was during this period that he played a leading role in CEPA—the Centro de Educación y Promoción Agraria—which had been formed to link together the various Rural Pastoral Outreach Teams and Delegates of the Word. CEPA was composed of both laymen and clerics, but they shared basic aims:

—To create the conditions necessary to form campesino organizations throughout the country;

—To foment an "evangelical liberation movement," in which the most fervent and responsive Christians would be trained to become community leaders; and

—To encourage these grassroots leaders to question openly the squalor and misery of campesino life.

The modus operandi of the Delegates of the Word, for instance, would follow a simple formula. Half of the discussions with campesino groups would center on issues arising from the Gospels, specifically, the life of Jesus and his struggle against entrenched power; the other half would involve discussions of Nicaraguan social reality, including an analysis of the importance of working people as the cornerstone of the economy, the unequal power enjoyed by the rich landholders as opposed to poor campesinos, and a definition of exploitation—what it is and how it works.

A key to the success of CEPA's efforts would be literacy training, followed up by making available publications, written in clear, simple language, so that newly literate campesinos would have the printed word at hand as food for thought.

One of the most famous of CEPA's publications was a magazine called CRISTO CAMPESINO, which raised eyebrows even with its first couple of issues. But when the third issue, devoted to inequalities of land distribution in Nicaragua, appeared, the uproar was immediate. Some bishops prohibited the magazine's republication in their dioceses for fear of somocista repression. Some in the church hierarchy accused CEPA of only being interested in social agitation at the expense of their "essentially and exclusively religious" mission. From the government came grumbling about "Marxism" and "foreign influence" that might lead to "unforeseen consequences." For Gaspar and other Catholic progressives, this was a sign that they'd hit their target.

His work with CEPA took Gaspar around the country and put him in contact with dozens of activist Christians like himself who were sowing new seeds. As his anger against somocismo grew, so did his sense that at least some campesinos were beginning to see what had been done to them, to understand their predicament, and to wonder how it might be changed.

Yo sé que llevas un estigma en la
    memoria
grabado con el hierro del ganado
campesino de América.

Te pusieron el hierro siendo gente
y quedó el sello de la esclavitud
como una herida sangrienta.

No dejes que cautericen la llaga.
recuerda la represión y los engaños,
recuerda la enfermedad en la carne
    de tus hijos,
recuerda el hambre y la miseria
    pavorosa
y recuerda la risa de sus bocas
sarcásticas.

I know you carry a stigma
burnt into your memory
with a branding iron,
campesino of America.

Those Decent Folks pressed the
    iron against you
and the mark of slavery remained
like a bleeding wound.

Don't let them cauterize the sore:
remember the repression, the
    deception,
remember the illness that struck
    your children,
remember the hunger and the
    fearful miseries,
and remember the laughter from
    their sarcastic mouths.

· · · 3

While Gaspar wrestled with stubborn problems in San Juan del Sur, Regalado faced his own difficulties in Tola. The traditional mid-December celebration of the Feast of the Virgin of Guadalupe had tended to be fairly secular in Tola, with parades, dances, fireworks, alcohol, and lots of noisy fun. But a sizeable part of the congregation of Regalado's church, taking their cue from him, wanted to focus on the purely religious aspects of the feast and use it as a time of devotion and reflection on the quality of their lives. Consequently, Regalado announced that the 1974 procession of the statue of the Virgin would be limited to the immediate environs of the church, rather than meandering its usual raucous way through the entire town. The traditionalists reacted violently, Regalado stood his ground, and in no time the more secular half of the congregation was agitating for his removal. They even took the Virgin out of the church and staged their own defiant procession following the time-honored route.

But this reaction had not risen out of nothing. Ever since his arrival, Regalado's style had chafed more prosperous and conservative toleños. For one thing, he had organized a cooperative composed of the poorest members of the community. When the group met, Regalado gave classes in social awareness and the poor responded rapidly with a burst of communal concientización. The younger members of the cooperative grew increasingly restless and impatient with the status quo. As a result of his ac-

37

tivities, Regalado was labelled a Communist by the traditionalists, led by the Torres family, prominent somocistas.

When news of this uproar reached the bishop, Monsignor López Fitoria closed the church and convened a special commission of four priests, including Gaspar, which met in February 1975. All sides appeared before the commission. Words were heated and the impasse seemed insoluble. But Gaspar, urged by the discreetly progressive Herrera family, offered himself in Regalado's place, with two stipulations: he would continue to live in San Juan, commuting to Tola as needed; and the congregation would end once and for all the divisive bickering. The factions agreed. Regalado and Gaspar exchanged parishes.

Now the white Renault made the run almost daily down the La Chocolata and over the hills to Tola at speeds that made the occasional passengers close their eyes and hold their breath. Despite his total agreement with Regalado's stance, Gaspar made a special effort to appear impartial, and tempers seemed to cool. When the next procession time rolled around, Gaspar permitted the traditional celebration. But he also picked up the campaign of consciousness raising where Regalado left off, at first dividing lessons equally between religious and social instruction. As the months drew on, however, the sociopolitical accent of his work with the campesinos grew ever stronger. The petty bourgeois opposition in Tola was not happy, and they staged a silent boycott of many of his activities. An uneasy calm reigned.

Gaspar's first year in Tola coincided with his deepening involvement in CEPA, so that what happened in his meetings with his poorer parishioners in Tola was happening in comparable form elsewhere in Nicaragua: the peasantry was slowly waking up.

Frequently, Gaspar's organizing took him away from Tola. One of his favorite themes in his talks around the country was God's plan for the liberation of the oppressed. He especially liked to retell the story of the people of Israel, their long struggle, their tenacity and solidarity, and their final victory.

Regalado, clearly relieved to get out of Tola, worked hard in San Juan and also assisted Gaspar in his work with CEPA and with a new committee, Pastoral Nacional Nicaragüense, of which Gaspar was a key member. While the priests agreed that Nicaragua was in need of fundamental change, they disagreed over the means.

Gaspar said he could see less and less chance for a peaceful solution. The outbreak of nationwide armed struggle was, in his view, inevitable. He told Regalado, "When the people—particularly the urban and rural poor—are ready in a couple of years, Somoza will be overthrown."

Regalado worried that Somoza's forces were far too well armed and if an uprising came there would be a bloody retaliation and the very young people they had been training would be the first to die. Better to struggle non-violently and wait for things to change, he thought.

Indeed, by 1975, despite sporadic reports of actions by the Frente Sandinista up in the mountains, an insurrection did not seem near at hand. And yet explosive thoughts were building up in Gaspar's mind. After a short retreat to San Jorge on the lake shore, he wrote:

CAMPESINO	CAMPESINO

a orilla del lago más bello del
  mundo
sentí más fuerte que nunca
el ideal que me inspiras.
	at the edge of the world's
	  most beautiful lake
	I felt more strongly than ever
	the ideal you inspire in me.

Te vi, gota con gota, lago inmenso de opresión profunda.	I saw you drop by drop immense lake of fathomless oppression.
Te vi azul con azul, espejo de Dios, en tu ser incoloro.	I saw you blue against blue God's mirror in your colorless existence.
Te vi entre volcán y volcán, cercada tu grandeza de opresores poderosos.	I saw you between volcano and volcano your greatness fenced in by powerful oppressors.
Pero vi que entre opresor y opresor había resquicios de esperanza que se podían romper con dinamita.	But I saw that between oppressor and oppressor there were little chinks of hope you could blow open with dynamite.

❖

Somoza kept a villa in San Juan—two villas actually, one for himself and his current mistress Dinorah, and another for his wife. When he came to town it was like a state of siege, the streets full of Guardia, whole barrios cordoned off.

His custom during his stays in San Juan was to make excursions out to the countryside to eat at some little farm ("All Nicaragua is my private farm," he was reported to have said) or visit the homes of friends and supporters. On one occasion, reported by Padre Manuel, Somoza visited Frank Kelly, a large landholder who lived just outside of San Juan. Guests included Dinorah, the infamous Colonel Ebertz ("Vulcano") of the Guardia, and a judge from Rivas, Jamil Herrera. What Somoza did not know was that Jamil's brother had secret ties to the FSLN, and that Jamil occasionally passed on information about Somoza.

Partly as a joke, and partly to relieve the monotony of the party, Ebertz mentioned to Somoza that Jamil was famous for his recitations of poetry. Despite his polite refusals, Jamil finally agreed to recite. He produced a moving rendition of "Penas y alegrías de amor," which tells the story of a man betrayed by the woman he loves. To Jamil's surprise, the poem rubbed some old wound of suspicion or jealousy in the dictator's mind. Somoza became outraged, Dinorah began to weep, and Ebertz whispered to Jamil that he'd better slip away. But as the young judge turned to go Somoza came bearing down on him and tried to boot him in the rear. Jamil attempted to avoid the blow, but Somoza managed to connect at least enough to fracture a little toe.

A few days later a cartoon appeared in *La Prensa* showing Jamil and Somoza, the latter with his foot in a cast.

Jamil did not forget the insult.

Gaspar made a new friend during his time in Tola, an idealistic young teacher from Toro Venado named Juan Brenes. In the long conversations that sometimes lasted late into the night, the priest and the teacher realized how closely they agreed on a number of things, and on one in particular: that Somoza was the key to the misery of Nicaragua. If he were suddenly removed from the scene, by one means or another. . . . Alas, no such likelihood. But suppose he were gone: would not most of the sorrow that afflicted Nicaragua vanish with him?

And so one night they came to the realization that they must kill Somoza on one of his next visits to San Juan.

Giddy with excitement, Gaspar communicated the idea to Regalado, who asked simply, "What makes you think you have the right to kill him?"

For days Gaspar meditated on this question. As Padre Ramón Pardina describes it, "It was a moment of real difficulty for his conscience. And so he began to read and re-read treatises of moral theology, because in general the Catholic religion does not allow murder as a way of solving problems. But the Catholic Church does admit that in an extreme case, when there is no other choice, it is permissible to kill a tyrant for the sake of the welfare of the people. He spent hours in the library, reading these books of moral theology, both modern and older ones, such as Saint Thomas Aquinas—to see if the proper circumstances existed in Nicaragua that would permit that choice. He concluded that, yes, the circumstances did exist, and that morally he could kill Somoza, without committing a sin, so long as it was for the good of the nation, for the people."

For Gaspar, to have reached the conclusion that tyrannicide was morally defensible meant proceeding immediately with the act: "Kill the dog, you kill the rabies," in the words of a Spanish proverb.

Regalado was skeptical: somocismo without Somoza was always a possibility.

"Maybe," countered Gaspar, "but a somocismo much easier to overthrow."

Gaspar and Juan Brenes pushed forward with their plans, studying the timetables and movements of Somoza's visits to San Juan. In the end, the only unchanging detail of his routine was that at the end of each (unannounced) visit, his car would pull away from the elegant villa on the tree-lined boulevard that faces the sea and, following a motorcade of Guardia trucks and other escort vehicles, head back toward Managua. The dictator's car was bulletproof, but not bombproof. There was—and still is—a manhole that could not be avoided by outbound traffic. Gaspar decided that they would plant the largest charge of dynamite they could manage in the manhole to be detonated by remote control. A lookout would be on the beach opposite the villa, pretending to be bathing. At the exact moment Somoza's car passed over the manhole, the lookout would signal the detonator and Somoza would die in a split second.

Gaspar and Juan had already collected the dynamite and reconnoitered the storm drain that led to the manhole when the FSLN, who learned of the plot, asked for a meeting. In the long discussions with Gaspar, the representatives of the Frente applauded the priest's motives but wondered about the results. Might not a vicious tyranny led by the upper echelons of the Guardia keep Nicaragua in a constant state of terror? Assassination, in a vacuum, without a carefully prepared mass uprising of a broad section

41

of the population who struggle together to change the system from top to bottom, could be counterproductive. Or worse. The repression against leftists after Somoza's death could be horrendous, and not being ripe for the final insurrection, the revolution could be dealt a fatal blow.

After pressure from the FSLN, Gaspar agreed to suspend the plot. But the FSLN was impressed by the priest's decisiveness, his meticulous planning, and his ferocious moral passion.

❖

It is not clear exactly when Gaspar first learned of the principles and goals of the Frente Sandinista. He must have gathered something from his discussions with the Frente about the assassination plot. Padre Manuel thinks Juan Brenes's friend Alvaro Miranda, an old leftist who had travelled much in Latin America, was a more direct source. He had been in Chile during the Allende years, fleeing to Nicaragua when right-wing forces crushed that experiment in socialist democracy. In Nicaragua, he joined the Frente.

Alvaro's contacts with Gaspar followed the classic FSLN pattern: get to know your subject well, cultivate him slowly, and when you know his mind completely, propose some simple level of collaboration. When Alvaro spoke generally about the aims of the FSLN, Gaspar asked for more information. Alvaro secretly brought him propaganda documents and position papers from the Frente. This was risky. To be in possession of "subversive" documents could mean signing your own death warrant. At any rate, Gaspar found himself in agreement with the liberating goals of the FSLN and made it clear to Alvaro that he'd be glad to help in whatever way he could.

As one of his first acts of collaboration, Gaspar welcomed the guerrillero Camilo Ortega to San Juan during periods when he needed to hide. Like his brother Daniel, Camilo was severely myopic and wore thick glasses, and with his timid, scholarly air, it was easy for Gaspar to pass him off as "Brother Chepe," a student preparing himself for seminary.

Gaspar and Chepe would spend long hours discussing the future of Nicaragua. And Gaspar would always make a point of including "the student" in the hikes and beach trips he took with his young parishioners.

During this period, one of Gaspar's missionary colleagues, Padre Luis, was expelled from Guatemala for organizing the Indians and was sent by his superiors to San Juan (where, after Gaspar became an active guerrillero, Luis would become the parish priest). He had scarcely unpacked when

Gaspar said to him, "Look, Luis, I've begun working with the Frente Sandinista. I'm trying my best to keep this separate from my religious work. I don't want to compromise anyone. So if you want, I can have my meetings with members of the Frente elsewhere. The last thing I want is to get you and Regalado and the others mixed up in this."

Luis assured Gaspar there was no need to worry. "We've never had secrets. Let's not start now."

And so Gaspar introduced Chepe, who became a fast friend of Luis.

So great was Gaspar's confidence in the trustworthiness of his fellow priest that on occasion he would ask Luis to do errands connected with his political work. Once, at Gaspar's request, Luis agreed to drive Chepe to Rivas. During the trip, Chepe showed Luis the two hand grenades he always kept with him. At La Virgen, where the dirt road from San Juan meets the Pan American Highway, they were stopped by a Guardia roadblock.

"Just be calm," said Chepe. "We'll be all right."

Luis began to tremble. The Guardia ordered him out of the car, frisked him, and questioned him closely. Luis glanced at the car. Chepe was smiling, his hands hidden under his cassock. Finally, the Guardia let them pass.

As they pulled away, Chepe drew out his hands, a grenade in each.

"I had them ready, just in case."

Only later, after "the student" had been killed in Monimbó, the Indian barrio of Masaya, during an uprising that signalled the beginning of the final move against Somoza, did Luis recognize Chepe in the photo of Camilo Ortega, one of the unquestioned heroes of the revolution.

Gaspar threw himself into his work in Tola with his usual energy. The focus was, as Padre Manuel puts it, on "the physical and spiritual health of the people and on the education and liberation of the campesino." His constant nagging of the Ministry of Education finally produced a promise of teachers and school supplies, but only if the schools were built to house them. And so Gaspar worked side by side with the campesinos to build a series of one-room schoolhouses. He saw schools as a crucial element in this project of concientización. The illiteracy rate was over 80 percent, and Gaspar understood the link between their ignorance of the world and their inability to judge things as they are, on the one hand, and their fatalism and resistance to change on the other. A campesino who could

43

read and think would be less likely to believe everything the bosses told him and accept the inhuman treatment his forefathers always took as "the way things are."

But when the schoolhouses were finished, the help from Managua didn't arrive. This meant more trips to the capital, more demonstrations outside offices, more anger and frustration for Gaspar, and more annoyance on the part of the government toward the uppity gadfly "foreign" "Communist" priest.

❖

The friction with local somocistas grew during an affair involving one of the largest landowners in the San Juan area, Carlos Hollman, who had a number of working farms and had bought or otherwise gained control of numerous other holdings—so many in fact that he was not always aware of what he owned. The zealous (but in this case naive) Judge Jamil Herrera, reviewing land deeds in Rivas, noticed that a piece of property in Miravalle on which 80 or so campesino families had been living for more than 15 years, actually belonged to Hollman. Technically, the campesinos were there illegally. When he next ran into Hollman, Jamil dutifully reported his findings; Hollman in turn ordered his lawyers to press Jamil to issue an eviction order. Judge Herrera, surprised by the upshot of his presumably harmless bit of information, resisted issuing the order. Hollman (through his lawyers) offered the judge 30,000 córdobas to expedite the case. And to cover himself in the event the campesinos got stubborn, Hollman arranged with Colonel Somarriba of the Rivas Garrison to have troops on hand the day of the eviction.

When Gaspar alerted the campesinos that they might be forcibly evicted, they announced that they would never leave and that they were prepared to die defending their right to lands they considered their own. And yet poor Jamil felt he had no choice but to issue the order. When Gaspar heard the order had gone through, he angrily called the judge.

"So young and already so rotten?"

"Mind your own business, Padre, and let the law run its course."

"The law! Whose law?"

Gaspar next wrote a bitter indictment of the judge's behavior to the Supreme Court, asking for an investigation. But Jamil made a smart move when he asked the Instituto Agrario de Nicaragua for a judgment in the case, pointing out that bloodshed in a land dispute in San Juan could ignite similar protests around the country. The Instituto reviewed the case, including the attempted bribery of a judge, and wrote a stinging letter to Hollman, demanding that he leave the campesinos alone, and stop trying to pressure the judge or he would lose the entire property altogether. Curiously enough, the Hollman affair brought Gaspar and Jamil closer together. They saw themselves as two men with different means, but with ultimately the same goals. The angry words they had exchanged seemed merely to clear the air.

❖

Late in 1976, an overworked, overextended Gaspar got a piece of good news: two Maryknoll nuns from the United States, Patricia Murray and Julia Muller, offered to come to Tola to lend a hand. Gaspar was elated. When he first met them, in Managua, he insisted on giving them a lightning visit to the area where they would be working. At breakneck speeds, he drove them south through the outlying countryside to Tola proper, showing them the new Centro Comunal that was under construction, thanks in part to a grant from the German charity Adveniat. He assured them that when they arrived to stay a month later the construction would be completed and all would be ready.

But in the interim things got complicated for Gaspar. The money for building the Centro Comunal ran out. Desperate for a solution, Gaspar arranged a public boxing exhibition between himself and the champion of Nicaragua, Alexis Argüello. Gaspar set up a ring and bleachers, and went into training. Word of the fight spread like wildfire. Tickets sold for 20 córdobas; the event was sure to be a smashing success. But on December 12, the day set for the match, with the stands full and the appointed hour at hand, Argüello did not appear. Feverishly, Gaspar phoned every place he could think of around the country looking for Argüello. No luck. The boxer seemed to have vanished from the face of the earth. After an hour, Gaspar cancelled the event. Instead of making a profit on the match, he was stuck with the expenses for the ring, bleachers, and publicity, which he had to cover out of his own pocket.

Less than a week later, Patricia and Julia arrived in Tola in a rented truck that contained all their books, clothes, linens, and other supplies. But Gaspar was nowhere to be found; they were told he was "off in the hills somewhere." Earlier in the day he had asked a boy to wait for the nuns, but the kid got bored and went home. And so the women sat down on their suitcases and waited. Late in the day, Gaspar finally roared into Tola and came screeching to a stop in front of the half-finished Centro

45

Comunal. When he saw the nuns, he seemed genuinely surprised and more than a little distracted. In fact, nothing was ready for their arrival—no rooms, no beds, nothing. He offered them the chaotic little hole in the wall where he occasionally spent the night, and mumbled something about stringing up a hammock outside for himself. But the nuns kept their spirits up as best they could and made do in the little room until a simple house could be built for them near the Centro.

Despite their bizarre welcome, Patricia and Julia grew to love working in Tola. They gave classes in town, helped in the church, and drove with Gaspar over dirt roads and across swollen streams, bringing religion, food, and medicine to isolated settlements in the hinterlands. They became deeply impressed with Gaspar's tireless dedication to the poor. But they also noticed his impatience, his touchiness, and his quickness to anger. It seemed to them he was being savaged by some inner pain that would not leave him.

❖

Early in 1977 conflicts with somocistas began to increase in intensity.

For over three years the somocista-controlled radio station in Rivas, "Radio Rumbos," had set aside a half hour, Monday through Friday afternoons and Sunday mornings for a program titled, "Voice of the Parish." Priests from San Juan, Tola, San Jorge, Belén, and Rivas discussed church news and gave inspirational talks. The program tended to be bland and noncontroversial until, in February 1977, the Nicaraguan bishops made public a forceful and incisive Pastoral Letter that analyzed Nicaraguan social problems and called upon Christians to help solve them. The newspaper *La Prensa,* which in those days was always in trouble with Somoza, published the letter in full, but the paper seldom reached backwoods communities like Tola, and besides, most of the campesinos couldn't read in any case. What little they knew about their country they learned by word of mouth or from the radio.

When Regalado took his turn on "Voice of the Parish," he announced that he was going to read the Pastoral Letter just issued by the bishops of the Nicaraguan Church. The station's regular host was surprised, but muttered something that sounded like assent, and left the studio as Regalado began to read the letter. Two minutes into the reading the entire station went dead, lights and everything else. By the time power was restored, Regalado's allotted half hour had expired. The host apologized for the inconvenience, but would not allow Regalado to continue with the reading—other programs already scheduled at this time, prior commitments, etc.

On Saturday, Gaspar called a meeting of all the progressive priests in the area and asked their advice. They decided that on Sunday morning Gaspar would try to read the Pastoral Letter without letting the station know in advance.

When Sunday came, Gaspar took his seat in the studio and as the program began, said in a clear, crisp voice: "Last Thursday we were unable to complete the reading of the Pastoral Letter of our bishops, apparently because of interference on the part of someone here at the station. Let's hope the same thing doesn't happen today, and that we'll be allowed to read the letter nonstop." And so he began to read.

The Radio Rumbos people had been forced into a corner: if they cut off the power again, everyone listening would know that this time it was no accident, and the priests would have won an even larger victory. So they let him read.

By six o'clock that evening, after consultations with Managua, the radio station announced that "Voice of the Parish" was being suspended indefinitely. The priests invited as guests had acted irresponsibly. They had turned the program away from its religious content toward subversive political agitation that could lead in only one direction, toward Communism. "We are sure our listeners understand."

❖

The Radio Rumbos affair took place just as another problem was coming to a head, this one rather more serious.

Gaspar had heard overlapping rumors about the goings-on at a big house in Tola that passed itself off as a hotel, but was in fact a brothel named "Luz y Sombra." He had delivered a blistering sermon against "white slavery" in Tola and against open defiance of the laws against prostitution. He had also accused the Guardia of protecting the owners of such illegal operations.

A week after the sermon, the issue blew wide open. Two girls from the brothel fled their captivity and hid in the house of a friend of Gaspar's. The girls were nearly hysterical; they were sure they'd be found and killed. But when they calmed down, they told their story: how they were both under 18, how they were locked in their rooms at Luz y Sombra, and how the madam had beaten them, burned them, and whipped them when they offered the slightest rebellion. They bared their shoulders and showed their

47

scars. Before, Gaspar had only had suspicions and hearsay to go on. Now he had testimonial proof.

Gaspar arranged for the girls to be housed safely, one in San Juan and the other in Rivas, but not before he and a group of his faithful appeared before Judge Jamil Herrera in Rivas to file a formal complaint against the brothel, alleging prostitution, physical abuse, white slavery, and corruption of minors.

Next Gaspar wrote to all the newspapers in the area, denouncing Luz y Sombra, and stating that girls as young as 13 had been forced to work there; that the madam had actually turned two of her own daughters into prostitutes; that girls who rebelled were struck with live electric wires; that at the first sign a girl wanted to escape, she was tied up all night to a chair; and that day after day the girls were forced to have sex with dozens of men.

Two days after the complaint was filed, Jamil appeared at the brothel, interviewed the girls, and presented a court order that the establishment close and pay a large fine. The madam paid the fine on the spot. But the next day, Luz y Sombra was open for business as usual.

Catorce añitos de edad	A mere fourteen years old,
dos de puta,	two as a whore,
cara joven,	young face,
rasgos viejos,	adult mannerisms,
piel lozana,	youthful skin,
ojos muertos.	dead eyes.
Pantaloncito ceñido	Tight-fitting shorts
desnudos piernas y ombligo	bare legs and belly
pies descalzos,	barefoot,
recorriendo el puterío.	back and forth in the brothel.
—¿Cuántos años tienes, niña?	"How old are you, child?"
—Señor, tengo diecinueve.	"Sir, I'm nineteen."
—Niña, tú no tienes tantos años.	"Child, you're not that old."
—Son diecinueve, señor,	She cuts him short:
ataja la criatura.	"I'm nineteen, sir."
—Mira, niña, soy el juez.	"Look, child, I'm the judge.
Si eres de menor edad	If you're under eighteen
yo te llevaré conmigo	I'll take personal charge of you
y serás honrada.	and make you an honest girl."

48

(Cruza un sueño infantil	(Some childish dream
por los ojos viejos	crosses the tired eyes
de la niña puta.)	of the child-whore.)
—Señor, tengo diecinueve.	"Sir, I'm nineteen."
El juez se vuelve hacia mí:	The judge turns toward me:
—Tiene miedo a la rufiana . . .	"She's afraid of the madam. . . ."
Catorce añitos de edad,	A mere fourteen years old,
dos de puta.	two as a whore.

❖

Que sí	Yes, of course
que la niña violada	the raped child
lloraba	wept
con desconsuelo.	in her desolation.
Que sí,	Yes, of course
que en su himen estaba	when her hymen was broken
todo mi pueblo.	so were my people.

❖

Once again Tola was split. there was actually a small demonstration *in favor* of the brothel, while some opponents talked of burning the place down. Things were getting tense. Colonel Somarriba, comandante of the Rivas Garrison of the Guardia, actually posted armed guards at the door of Luz y Sombra to assure it would stay open.

Gaspar increased his media campaign to close the brothel, bombarding the newspapers and radio stations with letters and offering interviews. But to no effect. When Jamil, accompanied by Gaspar, appeared at the brothel a second time, the madam merely laughed at them. "Look: I've paid off the Guardia. They're the ones that count. I have nothing to fear from you people." When pressed, the Guardia simply refused to carry out the judge's orders, even to arrest the madam.

Finally, someone in Managua, fearing a scandal that could not be contained locally, sent an order, and one morning a Guardia truck arrived in Tola, and in a matter of hours, all the beds, clothes, booze, girls, and other supplies were loaded up and carted away. By that evening, Luz y Sombra was open for business in Jinotepe, a town an hour north of Rivas.

49

Rosas jóvenes, negras	Roses young and black
piel gastada por el roce	the flesh worn out by
como cigarrillos apagados	manhandling
en bocas de borrachos.	like dead cigarettes
	in the mouths of drunks.
Amigas de la luna	Girlfriends of the moon
y del alcohol,	and of alcohol,
objetos enmarcados	objects labelled
en rutas de negocio.	"For Sale."
Autobuses que los monta	Buses: whoever pays the price
quien paga la tarifa.	can climb on.

❖

Shortly after the Luz y Sombra affair, Gaspar was driving to Rivas, and as he approached La Virgen he noticed a Guardia truck pulled over at the side of the road. At first he could see no one, but as he passed the truck three or four Guardia pointed their guns right at him. He sped away, zigzagging down the dirt road in a cloud of dust.

A few days later, returning at dusk from celebrating mass at Ostional, south of San Juan, he found the road blocked by an immense log. He stopped and got out, but heard nothing but the mournful call of the pocollo, the Nicaraguan equivalent of a whippoorwill. He got back in his car; and drove off the road into the adjacent field to skirt the obstacle. Then in the rearview mirror he saw a green Guardia truck swerving off the road into the field in hot pursuit. Gaspar jammed the pedal to the floor and bounced over the field, back onto the road, and sped off toward San Juan. The Guardia tried to keep up, but their truck was no match for the Renault.

A campesino from El Bastón named Marcelo, who had been trained as a Delegate of the Word and who often accompanied Gaspar on his trips working for CEPA, recounted a third incident to Padre Manuel. Gaspar, Marcelo, and the two Maryknoll sisters, Julia and Patricia, had left Tola heading for the CEPA office in Rivas when they saw a police car following them. Gaspar stepped on the gas and sped off, the car reaching speeds as high as 140 km/hr. By heading out the Pan American Highway north, in the direction of León, Gaspar lost the pursuers. When he slammed on the brakes and spun around back toward Rivas, Marcelo hit his head against the windshield, suffering a substantial contusion. The nuns were terrified.

One of them had been tossed off her seat onto the floor. Grinning broadly, Gaspar leaned back to help her up, saying, "O woman of little faith! If you ride with Gaspar you have to be a real man. Or if a woman, a real woman. Next time buckle up your seat belt."

But joking aside, Gaspar was shaken. He tried to think clearly. Obviously, the Guardia didn't want to kill him—they could have done that at any time. They were trying to scare him away, make him leave town, maybe leave the country. He had no reason to believe they knew he had begun to collaborate with the FSLN. Had they known that, they *would* have killed him. No: they saw him merely as a troublemaker in need of a bit of intimidation.

His friends in San Juan urged him not to return to Tola, but to stay with them where he'd be safe. Gaspar was unwilling to take so drastic a step, but he did begin to vary his hours of arrival and departure. And he began to make the Tola-San Juan run only in full daylight, "so at least if they decide to kill me, they won't have the excuse of having made a mistake because it was dark."

Sentí	I felt
la brisa helada	the cold breath
de tu mirada	of your watchfulness
sobre mi vida.	over my life.
Supe	I knew
que era rencor	it was your anger
por mi amor	over my love
al campesino	for the campesino

❖

In March, Colonel Somarriba called Gaspar to his office in Rivas for a talk. Gaspar had been saying in print and on the air that he was being persecuted, and the colonel "wanted to know the details." Somarriba was immensely cordial and attentive, encouraging Gaspar to expand at length about the attempts against him and why he thought anyone would want to do such things. Gaspar grew voluble and spoke at great length. But when the colonel was called out of the office briefly, Gaspar discovered— hidden under a cloth on the desk—a small microphone. Everything he had said was being recorded. When Somarriba returned, Gaspar abruptly announced he was leaving.

But Somarriba detained Gaspar long enough to make him an unusual offer: a squadron of Guardia to protect him around the clock, including his drives around the countryside. "One can't be too careful. There are so many . . . criminal elements around. And of course the last thing we want is an unfortunate accident like what happened to that priest in El Salvador . . . what was his name? Rutilio Grande, as I recall. Such a shame. I'm told the . . . ah, Mafia killed him."

Gaspar returned to San Juan deeply agitated. The death threat was veiled but unmistakable. Regalado and Luis counselled a rest. Why not a trip to Spain, until things quieted down?

Gaspar felt certain that the final insurrection against Somoza would begin soon, and the last thing he wanted was to be away from his friends and his flock when things began to heat up. Still, the suspicions of the Guardia were a threat not just to Gaspar personally, but to his contacts in the Frente. All right, he'd take a rest, a short one, but not without leaving a series of addresses and phone numbers in Spain where he could be reached if things came to a head in Nicaragua.

And so in April, Gaspar flew back to Spain, accompanied this time by his friend, the singer Carlos Mejía Godoy. Like the trip after the earthquake, the visit was fruitless in terms of arousing enthusiasm about Nicaragua among the brothers of the Missionaries of the Sacred Heart. Their indifference was all too obvious; the more passionate he waxed, the more their eyes seemed to glaze over. And Gaspar, waiting momentarily for a call that the insurrection had begun, felt himself curiously detached from Spain and its preoccupations. He was there only in body. Except for his family in Asturias, everything he cared most about was in Nicaragua, and it was all in imminent danger. The only politically successful encounter was with a group in Madrid who sympathized with the aims of the FSLN and who promised financial aid for the revolution. But all in all, Gaspar must have felt more like a visiting Nicaraguan than a Spaniard born and bred.

❖

Meanwhile in Nicaragua, the Bishop of Granada, Monsignor López Fitoria, called in the national director of the Sacred Heart missionaries, Padre Luis, and slapped a copy of the right-wing newspaper *Novedades* down on the desk.

"Look at this. 'Padre Gaspar García, the dangerous Communist priest.' And here . . ."

"This is no surprise, coming from *Novedades*," said Padre Luis.

"No, of course not. But this," said the bishop, taking a photostat of a letter from an envelope, "is rather more serious. Please read it. It's a letter written to a young girl who is interested in joining the Frente Sandinista."

Padre Luis read the letter. In it the girl was told, "If you've decided to join the Frente, get in touch with 'Angel' (Gaspar)."

"It's him," said the bishop. "I have other proof as well."

"What proof?"

"Rumors. Eyewitnesses."

Padre Luis realized that someone in the diocese, a fellow priest, had informed on Gaspar.

"You're his immediate superior," said the bishop. "Tell him I don't want him back in this diocese."

"Tell him yourself. Even if what you say is true, it's his own personal choice, and as such I respect it completely. I will not forbid him to return. I can guarantee that he has fulfilled his priestly duties to the fullest. And that's what matters. I will take no steps against him, and I doubt our superiors will either."

The bishop sighed and said nothing more on the subject of Gaspar.

Gaspar returned to Nicaragua in August 1977, but not before he had written a remarkable letter to the Bishop of Oviedo in Spain, outlining what had happened in the last nine months. This was clearly intended as a document for the record, in case anything should happen to him.

"My name is Gaspar García Laviana.

"I am a priest, a member of the Congregation of Missionaries of the Sacred Heart.

"I was born in the back country of Asturias, Spain, 8 November 1941.

"My father's name is Silverio García. A miner: 42 years in the mines.

"My mother's name is Enriqueta Laviana.

"I have been an ordained priest for 11 years.

"I worked four years in Spain and seven in Nicaragua.

"My passport number is 375. It was issued in Managua (Nicaragua).

"I have given seven years of my life to the campesinos of Nicaragua and I have committed no crime punishable by the law. I feel obliged to explain why the government of General Somoza wants to take my life:

"15 December 1976: I join delegations from 14 campesino communities for the purpose of demanding schoolteachers from the Nicaraguan Ministry of Public Education. We ask for an answer but receive none.

"26 December 1976: I lodge a public accusation against the Departmental Hospital in Rivas for their neglect of the sick, and for charging the poor unjustifiably high fees.

"2 January 1977: I lodge a formal accusation against the Government Office of Revenue, threatening to bring its head officials to court if they do not release unjustly accused campesinos.

"31 January 1977: I head for Managua leading delegations from 19 campesino communities, once again asking for schoolteachers. The Guardia Nacional refuses us permission to arrive in Managua. Despite that, we proceed to the capital.

"1 to 5 February 1977: I file formal accusations against two white slavers in Tola, for abduction, abuse of minors, corruption, and grave injury to public morality. The Guardia Nacional refuses to carry out the judge's order.

"6 February 1977: I read over Radio Rumbos the Pastoral Letter of the Bishops of Nicaragua, published in January 1977. The radio program is henceforth cancelled, and I receive indirect threats from the Government.

"7 to 18 February 1977: In my absence, the people of Tola gather a petition with hundreds of signatures, demanding the Guardia Nacional close the brothel.

"3 March 1977: The judge hands down a sentence ordering prison terms for the white slavers. The Guardia Nacional refuses to arrest the guilty.

"5 March 1977: I send a telegram to the Ministry asking that the sentence be executed.

"16 March 1977: The guilty remain free. I receive frequent death threats.

"17 March 1977: I send letters to General Somoza, the Ministry, the Archbishop of Granada, and the communications media about the situation in Tola and the involvement of military personnel in the case.

"21 March 1977: I am ordered to appear before the Colonel of the Guardia for the Department of Rivas. He reminds me of the murder of the Salvadoran Jesuit, Padre Rutilio Grande. He tells me to be careful, that the Mafia might kill me, and that I ought to accept guards at the door of my house.

"It was from this moment that I saw with total clarity that the Guardia Nacional was planning my death."

4

Sentí en mi carne
tu pobreza
como un látigo
de fuego.

Quise apagar
tu pobreza
con justicia legalista;
al no poder,
me convertí en guerrillero.

Campesino, abrasaste mis
entrañas
como lava derretida
en el seno de la tierra.

Quiero consumir el mundo
con los versos encendidos
que me inspira tu pobreza.

I felt your poverty
in my flesh
like a fiery
whip.

I wanted to undo
your poverty
with legalistic justice;
when that failed,
I became a guerrillero.

Campesino, you scorched
my innards
like lava melted
in the center of the earth.

I want to consume the world
with the flaming verses
your poverty inspires in me.

While no doubt sincere on one level, this poem oversimplifies Gaspar's difficult decision to become an active FSLN combatant. It is not merely that the "legalistic" system of justice had failed, but that certain key players in that system had come to see Gaspar as a threat, an enemy to be terminated. That he had become a marked man—or in Nicaraguan parlance, *quemado* (literally, burned) as one sympathetic to the rebels—was a crucial element in his movement from secret collaboration to open armed struggle.

As for feeling the suffering of the campesinos as a "fiery lash," I think we must take this as an honest, almost literally true, report of personal experience—especially coming from a countryman of Saint Ignatius, founder of the Jesuit order, who in his *Spiritual Exercises* encourages the reader to participate *physically* in the agony of Christ. When this poem was written, 1978 was fast approaching. It would be Gaspar's first year as a guerrillero, his peak year as a poet, and the last year of his life.

When "Angel" (as the Frente called him during his first period of collaboration) returned from Spain in August 1977, he put himself into immediate contact with the FSLN, which asked him to accelerate the preparation of young toleños and sanjuaneños for a general uprising. The overarching plan, which he confided to Regalado, was a simultaneous series of attacks all over Nicaragua: in every locality, the Guardia will be asleep in their garrison; two or three rebels will feign a street fight; a Guardia patrol will intervene, be overpowered, stripped of their clothes, weapons, and jeeps; the rebels will dress up in the stolen uniforms and drive into the garrison, disarm the sentries, and make themselves masters of the situation, seizing all the arms. Then—since almost every garrison in the country will have been overrun—the rebels will converge on Managua for the final battle.

Regalado, always skeptical, laughed. How could anyone believe such a complicated, cinematic scenario would work? But Gaspar had passed beyond quibbling into the intoxication of decisiveness. Of course it would work. It had to work.

❖

The inevitable showdown with Bishop López Fitoria loomed ahead during the upcoming conclave of all the clergy of the Granada diocese, to be held in San Jorge on the shore of the Big Lake. Regalado and Luis warned Gaspar that the bishop might try to expel him from his parish. "If he does, so be it," said Gaspar. "If he kicks me out, I go directly underground and join the struggle *en la montaña*. But the bishop is one thing; what about the Congregation?"

"Our tradition in the Sacred Heart is to respect personal choices like yours," said Luis. "I'd be very surprised if the Congregation tried to crack down on you."

The meeting in San Jorge went all morning without incident, but just before the midday break, Padre Santamaría, the local parish priest, took Gaspar aside and told him the bishop would like a word with him in private. When they were alone the bishop got right to the point.

"I want to know about your connections with these . . . Sandinistas."

To the bishop's surprise, Gaspar answered directly: "I belong to the Frente Sandinista. I've been a member for some time."

The bishop was silent for a while. Finally, he said: "This presents a problem."

"I know. And I'm aware of the possible consequences. I'm not just dabbling in this. My commitment to the Frente is substantial."

Again the bishop ruminated in silence. Then: "Have you thought about the possibility of . . . stepping down as parish priest in Tola?"

"Are you asking me to step down?"

"I didn't say that."

"I'm glad to hear that, because . . . Look: if I fail to fulfill my pastoral duties, if my membership in the Frente compromises you or my parishioners or my colleagues, then certainly you have a right to force me out. But if I haven't compromised you or the others—which I believe to be the case—then any action to remove me would be completely arbitrary."

The bishop sighed. "Well, let's see how things fall out, what 'possible consequences' ensue. But I beg you, commit yourself to no one. Not even to me."

Lejos de ti medito en
    la ribera
y afino mis notas discordantes
con las olas sonoras y constantes
que conocen la nota verdadera.
	Far from you I meditate on
	    the shore
	and tune my discordant notes
	to the perfect pitch
	of the sonorous, constant waves.

El lago recita la lección, ola por ola y blanco por blanco y repite y repite el mismo canto revolución, revolución.	The lake recites the lesson, wave by wave and whitecap after whitecap and repeats and repeats the same song: "Revolution. Revolution."

✤

During August and September, Regalado and Luis noticed a curious slacking-off in Gaspar's traditional "helping hand" approach to the campesinos. He seemed less and less willing to play the role of the all-purpose parish priest. When they asked him why, he answered that at this moment in the history of Nicaragua, to work steadily to ameliorate the conditions of the poor was in fact playing right into the hands of somocismo. "Think of Somoza's Nicaragua as a piece of clothing, a fabric. Everywhere you look it's unravelling. Why should I forestall that unravelling by applying patches? If all I do is help, help, help the campesinos they'll never learn how to help themselves. I'm tired of pulling their wagon for them. My job is not to make their lives easier but to make them see things clearly and get ready to do what needs to be done. At this point, awareness is more important than bread. I know that means temporarily more local, specific suffering. But that's the price we've all got to be willing to pay."

Nuestro mundo	Our world
es doloroso	is sorrowful
como el hambre,	like hunger
como el cáncer,	like cancer
como un año sin trabajo	like a year without work
como un racimo	like a bunch
de huérfanos,	of orphans
como una niña	like a raped
violada,	child
como un hombre	like a murdered
asesinado.	man.
De mi matriz	Out of my womb
desgarrada	ripped open
brota un tallo:	new growth springs forth:
es el mundo	it's the world
del futuro	of the future
que gestamos.	we're hatching here.

✤

The work that interested Gaspar most in these days was the training of Delegates of the Word. But not the old course of Bible study with a little social history thrown in. This time he spoke bluntly to the young campesinos: "If you want the kingdom of heaven on earth you're going to have to fight for it." He invited Camilo Ortega to address the group; Jamil Herrera's brother Hebert (a.k.a. Ernesto) also spoke to them. The young toleños were becoming a revolutionary cell and Gaspar was becoming their commander. By the end of September, they were spending time in the woods practicing the use of firearms and assault techniques. Finally, Gaspar announced that they had a mission: on October 13 they would attack the Guardia Nacional garrison at Rivas. Gaspar had been given overall operational direction of the attack; Hebert would be in charge of logistics. Their group of 28 men would be divided into two groups: one would neutralize and take the weapons of somocistas in Tola, while the other would intercept and disarm a Guardia patrol, seizing weapons and jeeps. Then on to Rivas. It is not clear whether Gaspar had decided to bear arms himself during this assault.

A shipment of arms was to be smuggled in from Costa Rica not only for the Rivas assault, but also for actions in Masaya and Granada. If, in addition to these three, successful attacks against the Guardia took place at other locations in Nicaragua, the Sandinistas would have shown Somoza and the rest of the world that they were a force to be reckoned with.

But the night before the attack, Gaspar arrived at the church in Tola where the combatants were gathered for the Rivas attack and announced that the arms shipment had been intercepted, jeopardizing all three planned attacks. Scarcely had Gaspar arrived when Hebert, already under suspicion, came to the door of the church just as a Guardia patrol was going by. The young people inside were on the verge of panic; some of them swore they'd commit suicide before surrendering to the Guardia, who were famous for their barbaric torturing of prisoners; others swore they'd fight to the last man, even though the 28 people had gathered only 12 old rifles and one pistol. Fortunately, Hebert thought quickly and after knocking at the door of the church, just as the patrol passed by and Gaspar opened the door, he said in a voice loud enough for the Guardia to hear, "Padre, the old woman who's sick told me to tell you she's waiting for you, and that you should hurry."

"Right away, right away, if I can just finish up here. Or better yet, why not tell her I'll come tomorrow. I have just too much work tonight."

The patrol kept going. The untested guerrilleros breathed a collective sigh of relief. Gaspar gave the order to disperse, one or two at a time, slowly, so as not to raise suspicions. But he was deeply disappointed at having to abort the mission: they were all marked men, but they had achieved nothing.

At this point in the history of October 1977 confusion begins to enter the narrative.

According to Padre Manuel, by the time Gaspar and his men were in the church waiting for the arms shipment, the assault on the San Carlos garrison had already taken place: "This means that all the other garrisons are on alert. Surprise will no longer be possible, but there is no rescinding of original orders. And so Gaspar decides to achieve his mission on the assigned day." This implies that Gaspar already knew of the San Carlos assault as he was waiting in the church and suggests that the San Carlos insurgents had somehow jumped the gun. Unfortunately, Padre Manuel gives no exact date for the night in the church on the eve of the Rivas attack.

But other accounts imply that all the attacks were planned to be simultaneous. Sergio Ramírez (Daniel Ortega's vice-president), for instance, writes: "The thesis set forth by Humberto [Ortega] was that the moment had arrived to effect an uprising in those parts of the population that had been militarily brought up to the level of 'vanguards' by the FSLN. There were to be attacks on the garrisons at Rivas, San Carlos, Ocotal, Masaya, and possibly at Estelí if the Ocotal attack succeeded—all on the same day." He doesn't mention the Granada attack, which Padre Manuel says was in the works.

When Humberto Ortega tells about that period, he increases the ambiguity: "In October, the enemy's schemes were totally destroyed, because at a time when they thought that sandinismo was dead, we were attacking Masaya, attacking San Carlos, attacking Cárdenas and Ocotal—and attacking offensively! And following that guiding military principle of conserving our forces." Others say Cárdenas was to be attacked by those who had successfully taken the San Carlos garrison; but that first attack was successful only for a couple of hours. There was no follow-up attack on Cárdenas.

José Valdivia, the Frente leader in charge of the October 13 San Carlos attack, says, "We met with two limitations: the attack had to be coordinated at 4:15 am, not before. The second problem was that they called us and told us the rest of the country didn't yet know about our attack—only the Northern Front knew. Then, there were problems with the messenger: he got cold feet, he got lost, he got the wrong house. There was no way to communicate with Camilo Ortega in Masaya, nor with Rivas, nor with Managua."

As for the Ocotal attack, Comandante Dora María Téllez points out that it collapsed when the seizing of a Guardia patrol was botched and turned into an ambush followed by a firefight. The Ocotal garrison itself was not attacked.

Bad planning, bad coordination, bad communication. The most anti-climactic episode was when the civilian group in support of the Frente, led by Sergio Ramírez, and including Arturo Cruz (later a prominent contra leader) and Carlos Tunnerman (later ambassador to the United States) decided to enter Nicaragua from Costa Rica and declare themselves a provisional anti-Somoza government. They rented a car in San José and headed toward the fatherland with their spirits high. But somewhere in the Guanacaste mountain range the car broke down, and the provisional government never made it to the border.

Whatever the facts about who did what when and who failed or who was misinformed or was to blame, the fact remains that one attack did come off as scheduled, and it is worth our while to take a closer look at the San Carlos group because of its similarities to the group that waited in the church with Gaspar the night the Rivas assault was cancelled.

By October 1977, the poet/priest Ernesto Cardenal had lived for 12 years in the Solentiname archipelago at the southern end of Lake Nicaragua. During those years, the consciousness raising of the campesinos of Solentiname included a literacy campaign; vigorous debates about the meaning of the Gospel (debates which Cardenal taped and published in a four-volume edition translated into seven languages); a painting workshop, which led to the creation of a distinct Solentiname style now highly valued by connoisseurs of "primitive" painting; and, early in 1977, thanks to a visit from Costa Rican poet Mayra Jiménez, a poetry workshop in which more than 20 newly literate campesinos began to write verse of remarkable energy and expressive power. Like Gaspar, Ernesto had come to realize that nonviolent means would never end the horrors of somocismo, and like Gaspar, Ernesto collaborated with and finally joined the Frente Sandinista. But unlike Gaspar, Ernesto never bore arms in combat.

With Ernesto's encouragement, a core group of young people from Solentiname suspended their poetry writing long enough to go into training for the October assault on the Guardia garrison at San Carlos, the mainland market town close to the archipelago. Most had never before fired a gun.

On the morning of October 13, the Solentiname insurgents caught the Guardia completely by surprise, fought a ferocious battle in the streets of San Carlos and up the hill to the garrison, and actually sent most of the Guardia into retreat toward the airport. But precisely because San Carlos was the only successfully staged operation of the day in the entire country, the full force of Somoza's Air Force was focussed on the young rebels later in the day and they were forced to flee. José Valdivia, known for this operation as "Comandante Zero," had neglected to prepare boats for escape, and during the scramble of the Guardia's counterattack, precious time was lost. Three of the young poets were captured: Donald Guevara, Elvis Chavarría, and Felipe Peña. Donald and Elvis were taken to a nearby hacienda, owned by Somoza, where they were tortured, shot, and buried. Felipe was imprisoned in San Carlos until the following August when the more famous Comandante Zero, Edén Pastora, staged his daring seizure of the National Assembly, holding legislators captive until Somoza agreed to free all political prisoners in the country. Felipe Peña was among those released. He and his friend Alejandro Guevara fought for a while with Gaspar on the Southern Front. Felipe also went on writing poems, one about Gaspar. Felipe was killed near Nueva Guinea shortly before the Triumph.

As a result of the Solentiname insurrection, the beautiful island community that Ernesto and his friends had built up over 12 years was burned to the ground. Most of its residents remained in exile in Costa Rica until the revolution triumphed, although a few—like Bosco Centeno, Iván Guevara, and Alejandro Guevara—fought on until July 1979. In 1979, Ernesto Cardenal became Minister of Culture for the new government. His first official act was to publish a collection of Gaspar's poems, *Cantos de amor y guerra*. Shortly thereafter the poems from Solentiname were published as *Poesía campesina de Solentiname*.

❖

For Gaspar, however, the cancellation of the carefully planned Rivas attack was a bitter setback. He too had been ready for action. But now that the arms had been intercepted and the San Carlos attack had taken place, the Somoza government began a serious crackdown on suspected Sandinistas. Gaspar was sure his name was on a list of quemados. By now

62

the somocistas in Tola must have gotten word of what all this coming and going of the Delegates of the Word was about. Gaspar was not only afraid, he was depressed. He decided he would leave Nicaragua forever. In the words of Padre Manuel:

"It was Gaspar's first and, we may say, almost his only defeat. He had been so sure of victory, a victory that would be achieved by a stroke of good luck, that the fiasco of the seized arms shipment and the cancelled attack plunged him into despair. What before was euphoria had now turned to total defeat. He no longer dreamed of triumph. Indeed, he felt that after this botched job the Somoza dictatorship would be that much harder to overthrow. Such was the nature of his spirits: from the greatest heights to the blackest pits. For him there was no middle ground."

He saw only two immediate courses of action, in this order of priority: flee the country or take refuge for an indefinite period—months, years perhaps—in the Spanish Embassy, where his close friend Vicente would protect him at any cost. To flee the country would require a visa, in this case valid for Guatemala. But Gaspar had to avoid showing himself at the agencies where such visas were issued. And so on their way to Managua, Gaspar and Regalado formulated the following plan: Gaspar would wait at a bar while Regalado tried to get the visa; in the event he was unable to get it, he would pass by the bar as a signal (in case he was being followed) and then call Vicente, who would come by in his own car with diplomatic plates, pick up Gaspar, and bring him to the embassy.

The ticket to Guatemala City was easy enough to buy; as for the visa, Regalado managed to find an agency that for a hefty fee would process Gaspar's passport and issue a visa.

It was 12 noon when Regalado's jeep approached the bar. He was sure he was not being followed, but there was no time to lose.

"Get in!" he shouted to Gaspar, who ran alongside and threw himself into the front seat without Regalado's having to stop. The plane left at 12:30. They were 15 kilometers from the airport.

But as they neared the airport, they were stopped by a long line of cars. Because of the Sandinista military moves the previous day, every border and every airport was being carefully checked for fleeing subversives. Each car had to pass through four checkpoints. Gaspar's heart sank. There was no escape.

"It's no use. Let's go to the embassy."

"No," said Regalado calmly. "It's worth a try." He stepped on the gas, and by zig-zagging in and out of the line and at times driving right over the field next to the road, he managed to insert himself into line just before the checkpoint. Drivers in the line were less than happy with his moves, and let their anger be known, but Regalado simply held the airline ticket out as the jeep approached the roadblock.

"I'm very sorry, Lieutenant, but my friend here has a plane to catch in about five minutes, and if we're forced to wait, he's going to miss it, I'm sure you see our predicament." Regalado smiled and nodded and the Guardia not only let them through, but radioed ahead to the other check-points to let the padres pass.

The airline had already paged Gaspar several times, and the plane's boarding stairs had already been pulled away when Gaspar rushed into the airport and up to the desk. In the very nick of time (the engines already revving up) the desk clerk called the pilot, and the ground crew swung back into action rolling out the boarding stairs. With a quick farewell to Regalado, Gaspar sprinted across the runway and up the steps into the plane.

5

In Guatemala City, Gaspar sought out Padre Josep Maria, a no-nonsense Catalan who was the Regional Superior of the Sacred Heart missionaries. The two men spoke at length about the dangers Gaspar had left behind and about possible options for the future. If Gaspar wished, Josep Maria could find him a position in Colombia. Or possibly Santo Domingo. The Latin American Council of the Sacred Heart would be meeting shortly in Colombia. It could be easily arranged. During all this, Josep Maria did not judge or coerce Gaspar, only suggested that there were alternatives to returning to Nicaragua. He knew only too well both the risks and the deep attractions of practicing liberation theology in Central America. Within four years not only Gaspar but Josep Maria himself and two other members of the order would be killed, three in Guatemala, one in Nicaragua.

The television news announced the failed uprising of the Sandinistas and reported that many leftists had fled the country for elsewhere in Central America where they were being sought by local authorities. Gaspar grew agitated. What had he let his brothers in Guatemala in for, dragging his notoriety with him into their midst? Why should they suffer for his actions?

His fellow priests tried to reassure him, but now that he was out of Nicaragua and away from the arena of immediate action, his doubts and fears began to assail him as never before. He must flee, but where?

Josep Maria suggested a religious house in Costa Rica. "Yes," said Gaspar. "I will go to San José. I will go into hiding. I will wait for word

65

from the Sacred Heart Council. Whatever they decide, that will be my future path. Of course, I prefer working with the rural poor. But whatever is decided, that's what I'll do."

And so Gaspar flew to Costa Rica, and shortly thereafter, Josep Maria flew to Bogotá to arrange Gaspar's future.

❖

Ahora	Now:
¡Qué negras las noches de mis días!	How black the nights of my days!
¡Qué oscuras las sombras de mis sueños!	How dark the shadows of my dreams!
¡Qué lejanas las promesas de mis frutos!	How far the promise of fruition!
Después	Later:
¡Qué radiante el futuro!	How radiant the future!
¡Qué igualdad entre la gente!	What equality between people!
¡Qué mundo tan diferente!	What a different world!

❖

Despite his sudden access of passivity, Gaspar was far from calm in his mind. Certainly, to leave Central America forever would seem to be a solution. Certainly, it was possible to imagine a life working with the poor elsewhere. But flying over Nicaragua could not erase it from his thoughts. Images crowded his mind: malnourished children, waves breaking along the lake shore, oxcarts heaped with firewood, an old campesino in his final hours gripping the priest's hand, flocks of egrets banking over the river that cuts through San Juan, the sun dropping into the western sea, and faces, voices—Regalado, Luis, Emilio, Catucha, all the others who had been changed by him and had changed with him. How could he leave all that, all those? True, Colonel Somarriba would still be there waiting for him. So would Somoza. But others had given themselves to the struggle for a new Nicaragua. Others were ready to live through, even die through, this difficult birth process. He had been preaching the necessity of taking that difficult path. It would be intolerable to become one of those hypocrites who gives advice he's unwilling to follow himself.

And yet he was still a priest, would always be a priest, and despite Saint Thomas Aquinas's elegant justifications of occasional tyrannicide, he, Gaspar, might end up with blood on his hands. Whose blood? The

66

tyrant's? Not much chance of that. More likely the blood of some young campesino desperate enough, brainwashed enough to join the Guardia. Whatever his choice, one thing was clear: now that he had been tagged as a subversive he could never go back to Tola, working both as parish priest and secret FSLN collaborator. Those days were gone forever. Now, he told himself, he must either return to Nicaragua and take up arms, or withdraw from the struggle completely.

In fact, as he soon learned, the situation was not quite so binary. He could do useful work for the revolution right in San José. The Costa Rican capital was full of exiled Sandinistas, more compañeros than Gaspar had ever met in Nicaragua. Many others who thought as he thought shared his clandestine existence in San José. He soon found himself volunteering to be a courier, or an emissary, or occasionally a transporter of materiel from one "safe house" to another. Of course one had to be careful, not only because of the alert Costa Rican police, but also because Somoza had his own network of spies in San José who kept close watch on the movements of the exile community.

This then is the picture we get of Gaspar toward the end of 1977, according to various informants. He is sleepless and nervous, undecided, often changing location, his whereabouts unknown to his friends for long periods. He experiences phases of gloomy doubt but then overnight turns vibrant with almost manic energy and optimism. His elusiveness is heightened by his frequent use of assumed names to keep the police off his trail: Miguel, Angel, Pedro, Pablo.

One incident recounted by José Raúl Muñiz gives us a brief glimpse of Gaspar's way of life during December of that year. He had left his private notebook in the Casa Cural in San Juan and sent word that it would be a great favor if someone could bring it to San José. So José Raúl, his wife Margarita, his brother-in-law Enrique Calderón, and Emilio all piled into a little Fiat and drove to Costa Rica with the notebook:

"We had only the vaguest idea where he was. We had phone numbers of friends, but nothing more. So when we arrived we went by a certain parish, asked the priest if he knew where Gaspar was, but he said no, so we went on looking, chasing down leads. We went to a school searching for a woman we knew about, Rosario La Fátima I think her name was, who might know of Gaspar's whereabouts. We identified ourselves to the Mother Superior, who said, no, he wasn't there, but yes, she said, I know him but I don't know where he is. We said yes, but we consider that we have a good reason to want to see him, and we know that his life here in

San José is clandestine, and that it's important that very few people know his whereabouts, but we are friends of his, brothers of his from back there, and we have this notebook of his we're supposed to give to him.

"So the Mother Superior called the nun we knew about, Sor Rosario, and she talked to us and it was obvious we were from San Juan and that we knew Gaspar and were really his friends. She said she would try to put us into contact with him. He's away right now, she said, but he'll be back, and what I need from you is the name of the place you're staying and the phone number so that when he returns he can get in touch with you. . . .

"And so the next day the phone rang when we least expected it, and it was Gaspar, and we talked, with one of the other compañeros on the extension and he said, meet me in the Central Park but don't bring your own truck, it's too well known by now, better you should find some other vehicle. And so we did everything just as he said, got another car, a Land Rover, and pulled up in front of the Cathedral, opened the door, and before we knew it a man got in. It was Gaspar. We drove away right then and there, and went to a restaurant on the outskirts of the city. It was about 8:30 in the evening, and we stayed there with him, eating and talking and talking until two or three in the morning about everything, about how the struggle was going back home, and we ate some more and we got back to the hotel about four and got a little sleep. . . .

"It was really a very beautiful experience, despite the fact that it almost cost us our lives when we crossed back into Nicaragua, because somehow the Guardia had found out we'd had a meeting with Gaspar, and they were waiting for us at the border. Things looked really bad, but, fortunately, one of the Guardia was a relative of one of us and we asked him to intervene for us, told him that there must have been some terrible mistake. He spoke for us and finally they let us go. It was really close. This was in December 1977. This was the last time we saw Gaspar, although there were rumors during the following year, when he was back in the country and in the guerrilla and moving around incognito that various compañeros had seen him—in various activities, in the country, in the town. . . . Once, a friend of ours, Rosa María, swore she had seen him going by in a car, she even said aloud, 'That's Gaspar! Right there!' As it turned out later he mentioned in a secret letter to us that, yes, he had seen Rosa María standing in front of the bank. . . ."

❖

Early in December, Josep Maria had sent a letter to Gaspar—addressed to an assumed name at a San José post office box—that the post in Santo Domingo was waiting for him. But no answer was forthcoming. As far as his religious superiors were concerned, Gaspar was invisible. But during the month of clandestine activity, Gaspar was thrown in with various highly committed militants, such as Camilo Ortega's brother Humberto, Alejandro Guevara from Solentiname who had fled to San José after the October attack on the San Carlos garrison, and perhaps most important, a woman named "Estrella," previously known as Soledad or Cholita. Estrella was the daughter of Napoleón García, who owned a filling station at the southern border town of Peñas Blancas, and who, because of his close contacts with the Guardias who controlled the border, was able to pass important information on to the Frente. Estrella had moved to Costa Rica where she was active in leftist politics, but her ties to the FSLN and her commitment to the struggle back home grew ever stronger. It was Camilo Ortega who asked her to seek out Gaspar that December, to sound him out—delicately, respectfully—about working for the Frente, first in an "apprentice" capacity, and later perhaps with a more direct commitment. Estrella's message was to be this: you did good work in Nicaragua, we can use you now, we'd be glad to have you with us, but the decision is entirely yours and you need to be completely certain when you choose to become one of us.

In fact, Estrella and Gaspar became close friends, and it was to her that he confided his doubts and anxieties, his inner turmoil about the choice he was in the process of making. Estrella was no stranger to what he was going through. Even for someone not committed to the religious life, joining the Frente was a difficult passage:

"We knew getting involved with the Frente was not something to be taken lightly. All our actions had to be thought of as personal, our choices private. No one was responsible for ourselves but ourselves. What's more, even though we might be misunderstood by our nearest and dearest, we could never talk about belonging to the Frente, except to those we were certain we could confide in completely. . . .

"People at my house had been thinking some pretty bad things about me for quite some time, because they saw me going out with different boys on different days and sometimes not returning home until late at night. Of course all that time I was working on secret missions, but despite the fact that a single word would have been enough to make them see they were wrong about me, I couldn't say anything, at least not until the people in my family had themselves become committed to armed struggle. . . .

"It was the same with Gaspar. He confided in his people up to a point, but he found it preferable to keep his commitment to the Frente secret from most people he knew. Of course it was true that the fear he had felt and the dangers he was facing were real. The attack [on Rivas] had been a flop, and it was necessary to assure the safety of those most deeply involved in it. The Frente had never told him he should return to Nicaragua, only that he should flee. And this is perhaps why he felt so discouraged in San José at first—this feeling that what he'd been working on had collapsed, and that the Frente had no further use for him. This is why he had begun to look for some other path to take. And he had decided that when the offer to work somewhere else came, he'd take it, because he didn't want to give up his priesthood.

"But meeting all the kids from Nicaragua there in Costa Rica, seeing that in fact the Frente was counting on him and did need him, revived his spirits, and he decided to resume his original path—only this time with an even stronger commitment, more directly involved. But this is also the root of the inner struggle he was never, ever free of and that made him such an enormously serious, even tortured, person—his sense of the incompatibility between bearing arms and blessing his flock with one and the same hand."

But as much as she might have wanted to steer him toward the Frente, Estrella fought to maintain her neutrality during this period spent in long hours of conversation with Gaspar. She was his friend, she would listen, but she would not decide for him. Padre Manuel thinks that Gaspar *was* looking for someone to tell him what do do (witness his passivity in leaving his future up to the decision of the Regional Council) and that meeting so many young people in Costa Rica who were ready to go home and fight for the things he'd been preaching about all along plunged him into deeper torment.

But Christmas was approaching. On December 22, he celebrated his 36th birthday. He became the local spokesman of the Frente with the Costa Rican press, and in the carefully arranged secret meetings with reporters, the man who had been known in Tola by the code name Angel, and as Miguel during his first weeks in San José, began to identify himself to reporters as Martín.

"Martín What?"

"Just Martín. That's all you need to know."

Finally, Estrella convinced him he needed a last name.

"O.K., Martín Martínez. Any objections?"

On Christmas, he called his family in Spain, telling them he was in Honduras and was well, and they shouldn't worry about him. He seemed to his friends calmer and happier than any time since his arrival in Costa Rica. He had made his decision.

❖

A short, slightly obscure vignette reported by Estrella: it's the end of December, she, Gaspar, another priest (unidentified) who has joined the Frente, and one other compañero have completed a mission involving secret arms and a safe house on the Costa Rica-Nicaragua border. It's night. They can see the lights of Peñas Blancas, Estrella's home town.

"Look, Estrella," says Gaspar. "Home. Want to drop in and say hello?"

She answers that of course she'd like to, but it's not exactly an opportune time. Gaspar laughs briefly, then falls silent. They head back toward San José. It is a sweet, still night. Estrella is in the front with the driver, Gaspar in the back with the other priest-turned-Sandinista. After a while, Estrella hears the two men talking quietly. She doesn't hear it all, only that Gaspar wants the other priest to hear his confession.

"I gave up doing that some time ago. I can't absolve you," says the other.

"But you're still a priest. Give me absolution. I need it."

Finally the other relents, and as the car rushes into the darkness, Gaspar whispers his confession.

❖

Anoche vino la paz;
ancló su nave en mi puerto,
y se paseó en silencio
junto a la orilla del mar.

Después se puso a cantar
una extraña melodía
al orden, a la armonía
al amor y a la amistad.

Yo le grité a la desdicha
que tiene postrado al pueblo,

Peace came last night;
she anchored her ship in my port,
and moved in silence
down along the edge of the sea.

Then she began to sing
a strange song
to order, to harmony,
to love, to friendship.

I cried out to her against the
  affliction

mordiendo el polvo del miedo, del abuso y la injusticia.	that keeps my people down, eating the dust of fear, of abuse, of injustice.
Cuando acabé de gritar, la paz habló de la guerra; y me dijo que en la tierra son hermanas guerra y paz.	When I stopped shouting, peace spoke of war; she told me that here on earth War and Peace are sisters.
Esto me dijo y se fue. Al mirar que se alejaba, vi a mi gente que lloraba. Y yo también lloré.	She said this and departed. Watching her sail away I saw my people were weeping. And I wept too.

❖

At one point in December, the Frente sent Gaspar up into the mountains in the north of the country where the Sandinistas had established what they called the Northeastern Front. There he met many young campesinos who had been trained by Evaristo, his Rural Pastoral Outreach colleague. To a man, Evaristo's Delegates of the Word had joined the rebels. He also was able to talk with the Ortega brothers, who of all the factions of the Frente were pushing hardest for an immediate armed showdown with Somoza.

We have only sketchy accounts of Gaspar's northern visit, but all agree he was surprised and buoyed to see dozens of campesinos, many of them brought to political consciousness by activist priests like Evaristo, armed, trained, and ready to fight.

If in the dark night of his soul he had thought of himself in isolated torment, he now saw once and for all that he was not alone.

❖

Certain bizarre myths have arisen about Gaspar during this period. One of them, popular in certain circles in San Juan del Sur, is that around Christmas 1977, the Sandinista leadership held a secret meeting on a yacht owned by Somoza that was anchored in San Juan harbor. Gaspar, according to the story, acted as moderator. During the meeting a Soviet submarine surfaced near the yacht. On it was Raúl Castro, brother of Fidel, who offered the insurgents Cuban aid in their attempt to overthrow Somoza. The Nicaraguans, goes the story, politely but firmly rejected the offer.

❖

As the year ended, Gaspar wrote two letters, both of which were published in major newspapers all over Central America (except in Nicaragua). The first was to the people of his adopted country.

"Nicaraguan Brothers and Sisters:

"During these Christmas holidays, when we celebrate the birth of our Lord and Savior, I have decided to address you as my brothers and sisters in Christ, and to share with you my decision to join the clandestine struggle as a soldier of the Lord and as a soldier of the FSLN.

"Nine years ago I came to Nicaragua from Spain, the land of my birth, to work as a Missionary of the Sacred Heart. I gave myself over passionately to the job of spreading the gospel, but I soon came to discover that the hunger and thirst for justice of those oppressed and downtrodden people whose priest I was, required the consolation of action rather than mere words.

"As an adoptive Nicaraguan and as a priest, I have seen in the living flesh the wounds of my people; I have seen the vicious exploitation of the campesinos, crushed under the boots of landowners protected by that instrument of injustice and repression, the Guardia Nacional; I have seen how a handful grow obscenely rich in the shadow of the Somoza dictatorship; I have witnessed an indecent traffic in human flesh to which poor young women are subjected, forced into prostitution by the powerful; and I have touched with my own hands the vileness, mockery, deception, and thievery represented by the power of the Somoza family.

"This corruption and repression have been deaf to all words, and will go on being deaf as long as my people groan at night surrounded by bayonets, and my brothers suffer torture in prison for the crime of demanding what is theirs: a free and just land, from which robbery and murder are banished forever.

"And so, seeing that our decent young people—Nicaragua's finest children—are at war with this oppressive tyranny, I have resolved to join up as the humblest soldier in the Frente Sandinista. I do so because this is a just war and one which strikes my Christian conscience as a good war because it represents a struggle against a state of affairs that is hateful to the Lord our God. And as the Medellín documents signed by the Bishops of Latin America point out, in the chapter on the Latin American situation, 'revolutionary insurrection can be legitimate in the case of a clear and per-

73

sistent tyranny which gravely offends the fundamental rights of the individual and deeply injures the common good of a country, whether the threat comes from one person or from clearly unjust structures.'

"I ask all my Nicaraguan brothers, for the love of Christ, to support the struggle of the Frente Sandinista, so that the day of our redemption will be delayed no longer. And to those who through fear or necessity are still serving the Somoza dictatorship, especially decent officials and soldiers of the Guardia Nacional, let me say that you still have time to side with justice, which means to side with Our Lord.

"To those businessmen who have not taken part in the corruption, to honest farmers, to professionals and technicians who reject the chaos and despotism Somoza represents, let me say that there is a place for every one of you fighting side by side with the Frente Sandinista to restore our country's dignity.

"To my brothers who work in factories, big farms, and workshops, to the artisans, to the homeless, unemployed, forgotten residents of marginal slums, to my brother campesinos, to those who work the harvest, crowded into camps, to the cane cutters and field hands, to those who've been robbed of even the most miserable chance to succeed in this land, let me say to you that the time has come to close ranks around the Frente Sandinista, to put our hands and arms together, because the sound of the guns of justice in our mountains, towns and villages is the sign of the redemption drawing near, because our common rebellion—the insurrection we will all carry out—will bring light, and drive away the darkness of somocismo.

"To my brothers in the Frente Sandinista fighting on the Carlos Fonseca Amador Northern Front, on the Pablo Ubeda Northeast Front, on the Benjamín Zeledón Southern Front, and in the centers for urban resistance, let me transmit my firm conviction that the day of our triumph will be built with the sacrifice of our fallen heroes, who embody our people's will to fight; with the revolutionary dedication of the people themselves, organized for the struggle; with the sacrifice we are ready to make in the trenches, united around the National Directorate, headed by—among others—Henry Ruiz (Brother Modesto), Daniel Ortega (Brother Enrique), and Tomás Borge (Brother Pablo), currently in Somoza's prisons.

"Somocismo is a sin, and to liberate ourselves from oppression is to liberate ourselves from sin. And so with rifle in hand, full of faith and love for the Nicaraguan people, I will fight to my last breath for the coming of

74

the kingdom of justice in our fatherland, that kingdom the Messiah announced to us under the light of the star of Bethlehem.

¡Patria libre o morir!

Your brother in Christ,

Gaspar García Laviana
Missionary Priest of the Sacred Heart"

❖

Despite not being published in Nicaragua, the letter was reproduced by various means and through clandestine networks made its way into Nicaraguan hands. The effect was immediate and profound. As Padre Manuel writes, "There is little doubt that this letter was Gaspar's greatest contribution to the FSLN. Not even his death, deeply felt though it was, had such an impact on the country. Many people say that with this statement Gaspar baptized the Frente Sandinista and made it loved by the people."

The letter not only spoke for hundreds of Nicaraguan Christians who had already committed themselves—or were about to commit themselves—to the struggle against Somoza, it also depicted a church militant ready to enter the fray, and not merely preach from the sidelines.

But was the Church really as militant as Gaspar wanted it to be? A clue may be gleaned from a second letter, less well known, that Gaspar wrote to his bishops and fellow priests:

"Brothers:

"The greatest contribution I can make to the Nicaraguan people and the Catholic Church is an open declaration of my unshakeable commitment to the Nicaraguan Revolution, which is most visible and active in the Frente Sandinista de Liberación Nacional (FSLN). I want you, my brothers, to be the first to know the motives that have brought me to this crucial commitment, because we have dedicated ourselves to the same vocation, and because we all sincerely seek the best way to serve the People of God.

"The state of ignorance, ill-treatment, and misery that most Nicaraguans suffer has made of our vocation a continuous and exhausting struggle to redeem our people not merely from individual sin, but also from the social sin by means of which the dictatorial regime of Anastasio Somoza keeps Nicaraguans on their knees. Our commitment to liberate them from ignorance and somocista oppression has made us enemies of the exploiters as well as victims of their repressive apparatus.

"We have suffered deception, calumny, every kind of persecution, even blows to our bodies.

"Our most active parishioners have been frightened away from belonging to our church organizations. Some of our Pastoral Outreach agents have been kept from performing their work as lay delegates among the people; others have been beaten and tortured in Guardia garrisons; still others have been accused of being 'subversives,' and have been tortured and then killed.

"Brothers:

"Was not Christ himself tortured? Is not the Church itself being murdered in each of its children?

"We cannot remain mute spectators before the tragedy of the people while the Somoza dictatorship, driven insane by money and power, goes on torturing and killing Nicaraguans as though they were animals with no rights.

"Brothers: I cannot remain silent before this situation, because to do so would be to help keep the brutal government of Somoza in power. This would only confuse honest Christians, who would never understand the cowardice of my silence.

"What is more, my faith and my membership in the Catholic Church oblige me to take part in the revolutionary process along with the FSLN because the redemption of an oppressed people is an integral part of Christ's overall redemption. By actively contributing to this process I signal my Christian solidarity with the oppressed and with those who fight to liberate them. We have here a nexus between a just revolution and the Church, and by participating I gain the right, both as believer and as priest, to play a part in building the new structures a triumphant revolution will bring.

"As individuals and as a Church we are at the definitive crossroad. The moment has come to decide. If we hesitate, it will be too late.

"With luck, the potent, fertile unity of the Church may even force the Somoza government to withdraw, vanquished, and in so doing we will erect a milestone in history, being the first group the Church has ever seen that fought in a Christian revolution to overthrow a murderous regime and constructed a new society in which the Christian ideals of justice, love, and peace were fully alive.

Comandante Gaspar García Laviana"

❖

The Church hierarchy greeted this letter with stony silence. As Padre Manuel points out, the Nicaraguan church sanctioned participation in the struggle against Somoza only when the triumph seemed inevitable, waiting in fact until 17 days before the Sandinistas marched into Managua. "If the church in Nicaragua has any rights as far as the revolution is concerned, it is not because of anything the bishops did. In their case, tradition overruled decisiveness. And this was not the only evil. Priests like Gaspar, and Gaspar himself, were in the moment of their rebellion treated like authentic rebels who could only bring ill to the Nicaraguan church. In the bishops, fear won out over the reality of the Gospels, which clearly state that if necessary you must give your life to defend truth and justice. There were very few priests who had the souls of martyrs."

Gaspar's order, on the other hand, quietly affirmed his right to make the choice he had made. Padre Cuskelly, the Father General of the Sacred Heart Missionaries, is reported to have said of Gaspar: "Has he done anything wrong? His posture represents a personal choice. Has he asked to leave the congregation? The congregation is a mother and never abandons or rejects her children. Gaspar remains a priest and a Missionary of the Sacred Heart as long as he wants to. And tell him for me," he said to Padre Josep Maria, "that the congregation does not condemn him, does not reject him, and respects his decision. Make that clear to him."

The political effect of the two letters was immeasurable. As Edén Pastora has said, "They were the best possible answer to Somoza's propaganda. After these letters, in the eyes of many people, the Frente ceased to be merely a bunch of vagabonds converted to international Communism who wanted the destruction of their own country. Thanks to the letters, many people opened their eyes and realized what a total lie the Somoza regime was based on because Gaspar couldn't lie to them. They knew him. He had never betrayed them."

❖

Cantaría para ti,	I want to sing for you,
campesino,	campesino,
una sonata de cuna	a lullaby
como se canta a los niños.	such as we sing to children.
Mi canción es un delirio	My song is a rapture:
mi canción	you are
eres tú mismo	my song yourself.

Mi canción es la verdad,
mi canción es tu destino;
yo te canto la victoria
y la guerra es el camino.

My song is the truth,
my song is your fate;
I sing you a song of victory
and war is the road that leads
     there.

6

Somoza's son Anastasio Somoza Portocarrero, also known as "Tachito," was part owner of a firm that made substantial profits by exporting blood plasma—this at a time when blood products were desperately needed in Nicaragua. When an exposé of the firm's practices was published in La Prensa, an enraged Tachito and his colleagues vowed to get revenge on the paper's editor, Pedro Joaquín Chamorro. Despite his origins in an established conservative Nicaraguan family, Chamorro's attacks on the Somoza dynasty—while far from being radical in their theoretical underpinnings—had been a constant thorn in the side of the dictatorship. On January 10, 1978, a hired killer gunned down Chamorro in Managua. Somoza the elder was not personally responsible, but the blame was laid at his feet.

The assassination was a stupendous miscalculation. Nicaraguans staged demonstrations, some of which turned into riots, and strikes, including a temporary economic stoppage by the business community which counted Chamorro as one of its own. The base of anti-Somoza feeling broadened overnight: peasants and merchants, bankers and Sandinistas found common cause and held secret meetings to plan the overthrow of the regime. The Chamorro assassination catalyzed the floating rage of a working majority of Nicaraguans.

In San Juan del Sur, residents organized a silent march through the streets of the town to honor Chamorro, whose family owned a house on the hill overlooking the sea. The Guardia from the Rivas garrison was out in force, in full combat gear, but did not attempt to block the march. When the marchers finally reached the park in front of the church, the pealing of the huge bell in the steeple broke the tense silence. The big doors to the church were bolted closed, and the Guardia commander ordered his men to break them down to stop the bell ringing. The bell rang on. In frustration, the commander told a squad to open fire on the bell, to sever the rope, whatever was necessary to restore the silence. Shots rang out; many of the marchers screamed and fled; but the bell rang on. Finally, the door opened, the bell stopped ringing, and the two boys who had pulled the rope again and again escaped out of the back of the church.

❖

About the time of the San Juan incident, two former priests of that very church were having what was to be their last meeting. Gaspar was not the only one to have undergone a radical change. Regalado had fallen in love with a woman in San Juan and had left the priesthood to marry her; Regalado and his new wife had made their home in San José, Costa Rica.

According to Regalado (who has spoken to Padre Manuel about this last farewell), Gaspar spoke enthusiastically about his decision to take part in the armed struggle against Somoza, but it was obvious to his friend that "the priest-guerrillero contradiction was still weighing heavily on his soul."

Regalado was never one to mince words. He reminded Gaspar that one consequence of taking up arms could be death. Gaspar answered that he had no fear of death; if he was fated to die in combat, his only regret was that he would not be around to see the final triumph.

Regalado gave Gaspar a key to his house in San José: "For you or your compas [short for compañeros], whenever you need it." The two old friends embraced, then went their separate ways.

❖

MORIR

—¿No es mala suerte?
—No es mala suerte, no,
no es mala suerte.
Porque creo en la vida de la muerte,
el morir, para mí, no es mala
    suerte.

TO DIE

"It's not bad luck?"
"No, it's not bad luck,
it's not.
Because I believe in the life
    hidden in death,
dying, for me, is not bad luck."

❖

About a month after the Chamorro assassination, the residents of an Indian barrio named Monimbó, in the city of Masaya, decided to hold a commemorative mass and name a small plaza after their fallen hero. When the Guardia tried to break up the ceremony, the residents responded with rocks and fireworks and drove the Guardia out of the barrio. Stunned, then jubilant at their success, the Indians sealed off Monimbó with barricades and declared it "free territory." When the Guardia attempted on several occasions to re-enter the area by night, they were driven back by more stones, Molotov cocktails, and a few old guns. The only Sandinista organizer who arrived to lend a hand with strategy was the man known in San Juan del Sur as "the student, Chepe," Camilo Ortega. Monimbó held out for an amazing two weeks until the Guardia began bombarding the neighborhood with air strikes and with artillery from the top of a nearby hill named Coyotepe. But resistance continued, and only after savage house-to-house combat was Monimbó subdued. Camilo Ortega and 200 barrio residents died. But this first urban insurrection set a model that would be followed by other poor barrios in towns all over Nicaragua.

❖

For years the Frente Sandinista had been divided into three factions, each with its own tactics for overthrowing Somoza. The first group, the "Proletarios," followed a traditional and rather doctrinaire Marxist line: emphasize class warfare, organize the urban poor and factory workers, politicize the people and prepare them for armed struggle. The Proletarios were those most surprised to discover the people of Monimbó perfectly capable of insurrection without being prepared in advance by university-trained Marxists. Jaime Wheelock, Luis Carrión, and Carlos Núñez were the best known members of this group.

The second faction went by the name "Guerra Popular Prolongada," and took a long-term, patient approach: rural and urban workers would be brought slowly to consciousness; human and material resources would be marshalled carefully over the years; and military confrontations with the Guardia would be avoided until the moment was ready. Tomás Borge, Bayardo Arce, and Henry Ruiz were prominent in this group.

The third faction, or "Terceristas," called for immediate insurrections which would galvanize all sectors of the population; frequent hit-and-run

81

engagements with the Guardia; and ideological heterodoxy. The Terceristas—represented by Daniel and Humberto Ortega, Edén Pastora, and Víctor Tirado—attracted many students, radical campesinos, bourgeois reformers-turned-radical, and politicized Christians like Gaspar. And it was the Tercerista position that gained most legitimacy from the Monimbó uprising.

In any case, the factions had a common purpose and in 1978 and 1979 the differences between them seemed less and less important. In the wake of the Chamorro assassination, the scattered units of the Southern Front decided to join together in late February for attacks on strategic southern towns: Sapoá, Peñas Blancas, Rivas, and Granada. Overall command was put in the hands of Edén Pastora, who in turn appointed Gaspar "politico-military coordinator" of the campaign. For the first time Gaspar, dressed in camouflage, wearing a black beret and carrying a gun, would see armed action. And when the 80 or so guerrilleros were divided into two groups, one headed for Peñas Blancas and the other for Rivas, Martín (as Gaspar was now called) chose the latter. Colonel Somarriba had been replaced by Colonel Ebertz, but the Guardia was still the Guardia. Gaspar would get a second chance to confront them in their lair.

❖

Cuando llega mi crecida,	When my flood tide arrives,
la gente mira su empresa.	people see what it's able to do.
Ve pasar el agua brava.	They see the rough water rush by,
Ve removerse la tierra.	they see the old lands disappear.
Y se embarcan en mis olas,	And they set forth on my waves,
y sacuden la pereza,	and they shake old laziness off,
y el río los lleva lejos,	and the river carries them out,
flotando sobre mis fuerzas.	floating far away on my force.

❖

When various accounts of the 1978 Rivas assault are combined, the operation takes on a tragicomic quality.

Having secretly crossed the Costa Rican border, the Rivas contingent marched toward a spot on the Pan American Highway where they were to rendezvous with their transportation: a large truck that a young woman (possibly Estrella?) had rented under the pretext of moving furniture. Her plan was to feign sudden illness, ask the driver to stop (at the appointed place) and wait until the compañeros emerged from the bushes to seize the truck. But the attack force had miscalculated the time needed for the march; the young woman moaned and groaned as long as she could, but after an hour or so, with no sight of her comrades, she was forced to leave. When Gaspar, Pastora, Alejandro Guevara, and the others finally arrived, there was no truck.

They decided to improvise: They stopped the first vehicle that came along, in this case a group of Salvadoran trucks, commandeered them, and headed north. Within a couple of kilometers they ran into their first Guardia patrol. By driving along the shoulder and then opening fire, they were able to wipe out all three members of the patrol, although one compa was killed.

Gaspar shouted to Alejandro: "Well, there go four!"

Alejandro: "What do you mean? Where?"

Gaspar: "To heaven, hombre, to heaven!"

At La Virgen, where the road to San Juan cuts off to the left, and where the Guardia had once tried to ambush Gaspar, the rebels occupied the Hotel Gilmore. The proprietress greeted them with open arms: seeing their olive drab uniforms, she assumed they were Guardia. "Come in, Come in, Welcome! I know your commander, Colonel Ebertz—a great friend of mine. I always pay my quota. I'm all paid up, no problem. Welcome!"

At this point Gaspar, who had been listening from the next room, entered: "You're no friend of ours."

Her eyes grew large: "Padre! What are you doing here?"

"Father me no Fathers! You're a bunch of corrupt somocistas!"

They took the keys to all the vehicles parked at the hotel, broke the group into smaller units, and headed toward Rivas. Halfway there they saw a larger patrol—15 men—approaching, and opened fire. The Guardia scattered and the rebels drove on.

By the time they arrived in Rivas it was almost midnight. They spread out, according to plan, and at 2:00 am began the attack. Things went smoothly as they swept through town; what few Guardia they encountered fled to the garrison. Gaspar could be heard shouting to the inhabitants, who peeked out fearfully from behind shutters, "We're fighting for you! Come on! Join us!" No one from Rivas did, but 18 young people from San Juan and Tola joined them, committed to fight with the attack force and then return with them to Costa Rica.

According to Pastora, Gaspar carried some homemade pipe bombs. Alejandro lit one and Gaspar ran down the street and threw the bomb over the wall into the courtyard of the garrison. At least he thought it was the garrison. But when the bomb went off, Pastora heard the cries of women, screams and prayers, and the squawking of chickens. Gaspar had already thrown a second bomb when Pastora shouted, "What in the world are you doing?"

"I think I got the dirty crooks."

"You think they've got chickens in the garrison?"

Gaspar had been bombing a private house that looked a good deal like the garrison. By sheer luck, no one was seriously injured.

They pushed on. As they neared the garrison, they split into two groups: Pastora's would circle the compound and approach from the west, Gaspar's group from the east. But in the darkness, the two groups bumped into each other and when Gaspar saw uniforms that looked like those of the Guardia, he gave the order to open fire: "Let them have it! Get the sons of bitches!"

The others jumped for cover, and after the first hail of bullets Pastora cried: "Martín! It's me, you fuck-up!"

"Identify yourself!" shouted Gaspar.

"Martín! You idiot, it's me!"

Now that they had stopped trying to kill each other, they concentrated on the garrison. Each member of the attack force had been given 400 rounds of ammunition and was expected to save half for a final assault on the compound. They had one .50 caliber machine gun that had been firing steadily but suddenly fell silent. The gunner, Francisco, Gutiérrez, had been killed with a single shot. (It was later discovered that the .50 caliber had been beyond its effective range in any case.)

It was 5:30 in the morning.

"What do we do now?" asked Gaspar. "It'll be light soon. By now they know in Managua. That means the Air Force."

"Hold positions! Keep firing!" shouted Pastora.

"With what bullets? I think we're just about out."

Gaspar made a quick check of the others: he was right. There was not enough ammunition left for a final assault. Pastora gave the order to retreat. In their stolen vehicles, still firing from time to time, they roared through Rivas and headed south.

The Peñas Blancas attack had also failed to capture the garrison. But the guerrilleros of the Benjamín Zeledón Southern Front had made a bold statement.

There had been several casualties among the attackers, but one of them struck Gaspar with particular force: a young man called "El Guardita," who had served in the Guardia for a time, resigned, and had gone to live in Costa Rica with his wife. It was Gaspar himself who had approached the young exile and had convinced him to join the struggle against Somoza. El Guardita had been cut down in the street. When Pastora checked him out and saw he was dying, he called out to Gaspar: "Martín! Quick! Give him absolution." But by the time Gaspar got to him it was too late. As he wept there in the darkness by the body, he remembered clearly that day in Punta Arenas and the young man's words to his wife when the moment of decision had arrived: "Get my shirt ready. I'm going with the padre."

❖

La tristeza de tu suerte
me ciñe en el corazón.
Tú te fuiste con la muerte
y me dejaste el dolor.
¡Qué dolor,
guerrillero
compañero,
qué dolor!

El día que tú te fuiste
nació la revolución.
Este pueblo que quisiste
vio la muerte y no entendió.
¡No entendió,
guerrillero
compañero,
no entendió!

The sadness of your fate
encircles my heart.
You went away with Death
and left me the grief.
What grief,
guerrillero
compañero,
what grief!

The day you went away
the revolution was born.
The people, whom you loved,
saw your death but didn't
understand.
They didn't understand,
guerrillero
compañero,
they didn't understand!

❖

Abandoning the vehicles near the border, the attackers fled over treeless hills and through thick forests into Costa Rica. But even out of Nicaragua they were not safe. The Costa Ricans, who were capable at times of looking the other way when Nicaraguan exiles used the border region as a staging area, had decided to arrest as many Sandinistas as they could. Gaspar and some of his friends took temporary refuge in a convent in La

Cruz run by a close friend and sympathizer, Sor Marta. But shortly after their arrival, word came that the police might make a check on the convent. Gaspar and a couple of the others left La Cruz and managed to hide in an isolated settlement near La Libertad. They were stuck there for three days in a steady rain, hungry, exhausted, and anxious. Finally, Gaspar sent Sor Marta a note: they had to get out before people got too suspicious: It was election time in Costa Rica: might she not find a way to pick them up in a vehicle decked out to look like a campaign truck? She did exactly that: the truck arrived with signs and banners for the Liberation Party, and as they made their way back to La Cruz, Gaspar took great pleasure in waving a flag and shouting campaign slogans every time they went through a town.

Within days they were back in San José, where Gaspar and Alejandro resumed work, secretly delivering arms to the border area, whence they could be smuggled into Nicaragua, or training new recruits up in the mountains.

❖

Andaba persiguido como un perro
o como un tigre peligroso
o como un garrobo indefenso.

Lo perseguían
por matar a un asesino
que era guardia.

Iban guardias y guardias,
carros de acero,
pistolas, metralletas,
bayonetas,
porras y perros;
todos la misma cosa:
engranajes
de la maquinaria represiva.

Eran perros
que querían vengar
al perro muerto.

He ran, pursued like a dog
or like a dangerous tiger
or like a defenseless garrobo.

They were after him
for killing a killer
who happened to be a guardia.

They sent out guardias and more
   guardias,
armored cars,
pistols, machine guns,
bayonets,
clubs and dogs—
all the same thing:
cogs
in the machinery of repression.

They were dogs
who wanted vengeance
for the dead dog.

86

Por el monte,	Up in the mountain,
el bosque dejaba ir al guerrillero,	the forest let the guerrillero pass,
y las hojas no hacían ruido,	and the leaves made no sound,
de miedo.	for fear.

❖

Edén Pastora gives us a very vivid portrait of Gaspar during this period: "Courage consists of conquering fear, and I have known only one person who never showed fear: Gaspar. He bordered on the foolhardy and I was always trying to get him to cool it.

He always wanted to finish the thing, now, right away, as though he knew that the longer the victory was put off, the greater the chance he'd never see it, which was in fact how it turned out. All his actions were high speed, full throttle, as though death weren't dogging his steps. I never saw him give up or retreat. For him, the bullets of the somocistas couldn't harm him—that's what he told his compañeros.

"During the attack on Rivas I had to slow him down: 'Take it easy, Gaspar. It's all going to work out. Just let time take its course.'

"He viewed the Guardia with hatred, not an unhealthy hatred of individuals, but rather of what they represented. They were responsible for gambling and prostitution, two of the evils that kept Nicaragua plunged in the most abject misery.

"It was common to see him absorbed in his thoughts. So as not to bother the others, he'd go off alone, stretch out on the ground or lean against a tree, and just think and think. And often, later, he'd write. I suppose it was his thoughts, or maybe those poems I learned later he'd been writing. But he was very private about his inner life and he never let anyone see what he'd been writing. . . .

"But at the same time, he was happy, a live wire. He'd sing, he'd laugh. He was very open. His sense of justice verged on the perfectionist. This came from the religious and humane education he'd been given. That's where his discipline came from. Unlike others, for him what the commanding officer said was law, and he never deviated an iota from what had been ordered. In this he showed his great sense of responsibility.

"He had a great capacity for work. He was never tired, or if he was, he never showed it."

❖

Subiendo se va por el camino que camina en la montaña.	He goes on up the road that travels through the mountains.
Las agujas de los pinos le van hiriendo la cara.	The pine needles keep wounding his face.
Taladrando la espesura pasa el camino el viajero, acostando su figura con los paisajes más bellos.	Piercing the woods' thickness the traveller goes along the road mingling his form with the loveliest landscapes.
Y, cuando llega a la cumbre, no se queda en su cabaña porque el camino descubre que caminando descansa.	And when he reaches the top he does not linger in his mountain getaway, for the road has shown him that it's restful to keep moving.

❖

A vignette from Edén Pastora: the guerrilleros are training in the mountains of Costa Rica. Some of the newly arrived kids are sure Gaspar won't be able to endure the rigors of the long march they're about to take: he's too old, he smokes too much, he won't last. So a group of them challenges him to a race up over the mountain and down the other side. Smiling ironically, he accepts. He knows they've felt the prestige he enjoys and they want to test it. The race begins, the young men dash off, Gaspar follows, but at the finish line it is Gaspar who crosses first. "What made them think they could lick this old Asturian mountaineer?" he asks.

✧ ✧ ✧ 7

"There is a contradiction, an unresolvable difference between a dogmatic priest and a dogmatic Marxist. They are irreconcilable. But between a post-Vatican II priest and a Marxist who vitally lives the reality of Central American history, there is no barrier, no 'Church as opiate of the people'; there is rather the Church as a goad, a spur to the people. In America, in the realm of action, there is no contradiction whatsoever. . . .

"Europe is for people who want to spend their time theorizing. America is for life as it is lived, for putting things into practice; there are no dogmatisms in America. In this continent we don't sit around in cafes discussing theory. The theories of the Frente are born from actual practice in the real world."

—Fernando Cardenal

Gaspar, who had entered the service of the FSLN as "just one more foot soldier," rose quickly in the ranks. He was dependable, disciplined, a quick study. He also inspired confidence and a sense of values in the young fighters who worked with him. For some, like Edén Pastora, having Gaspar share their lives and their struggle meant taking a fresh look at their Christianity. As Pastora tells us:

"It's to Gaspar I owe my faith—which I had never really lost, thanks to my studies with the Jesuits—but which I had more or less buried because of certain external events which had nudged me toward no longer believing in the institutionalized Church. In the 1950s and 1960s, Nicaraguan clerics were for the most part corrupt, especially the leadership. They were all somocistas. When Somoza gave banquets up on 'The Hill' in Managua, the upper echelons of the Church hierarchy were always there. And the day after these parties you could read their names in *Novedades*. Only two bishops were opposed to this state of affairs: Monsignor Calderón of Matagalpa and Monsignor Padillas of León. The rest were drawn in to bow down at the feet of Somoza, even a large number of ordinary clergy. It was a disgrace for the Church. It made those who loved justice doubt their faith. It made you ashamed to say you were a Catholic. You mustn't forget that the Church gave full honors to Tacho's father—to a murderer, who was buried with full ecclesiastical rites.

"But meeting priests like Gaspar, you suddenly felt yourself turning back to your old original faith. You came to know a new Church: of the people, of the poor, the authentic Church of Christ, son himself of a campesina.

"Gaspar taught us this new Christ. Not the meek, gentle Christ 15-year-old girls dream of. . . . Gaspar always spoke of everyone's Christ, the artisan, his complexion darkened by sunburn, Christ with his hair roughed up by the desert winds, Christ with class consciousness, since 11 of his disciples were working-class. . . . He told us about a Christ who spoke of the struggle of father against son and son against father; of a Christ who tells you you have to fight otherwise they'll starve you to death; of a Christ who calls those blessed who fight—and he doesn't say how—to establish justice; of a Christ of the poor, who says it's easier for a camel to pass through the eye of a needle than for a rich man to get to heaven. . . .

"For him, to practice both Christianity and revolution was a difficult thing, since many are called in that direction, but few decide to act, because they're made fearful by the false counsel of 'conscience' or by 'what people may say.' Gaspar had risen above all this, or at least he fought as though he felt none of these hesitations. Once, he said to me, 'Edén, Christianity can never be against revolutionaries, nor revolutionaries against Christianity. Both preach love, freeing yourself from the material, love for morality and sacrifice for the sake of others.'

"Who says he stopped being a priest? I can tell you, many were the times he said mass in safe houses. I often saw him praying. Often! And a man who prays is a man sure about his vocation."

It was during this period that Gaspar told his friend Joaquín: "I've found in the Frente what I seldom found among my own people: the kids in the Frente give their lives for each other. I've seen how these compas are capable of dying to save a buddy. I've seen kids remain behind, in position, specifically to allow their friends to retreat. And they *knew* they were going to die. . . . Ay, brother! Now I understand what it means to be a Christian. These compas are teaching me plenty!"

The image of falling in combat is never far from his thoughts. But death is always seen as part of a larger destiny, a meaningful process of transformations:

Amigo,	Friend,
te darán muerte	they will put you to death
como en los tiempos del Romano	as in the time of the Roman
Imperio.	Empire.
Serás triturado como trigo,	You'll be crushed like wheat,
hecho harina para Cristo,	made flour for Christ,
para el mundo.	for the world.
Pan verdadero.	True bread.
Más, no temas.	Fear nothing more.
Será la gran persecución	There will be great persecution,
que colmará la ira de Dios.	and God's wrath will overflow.
Después vendrá el fin de las cosas.	Then will come the end of things.

❖

Because of bungling, poor strategy, and miscalculations in various actions—the Rivas attack among them—the Frente decided that certain key guerrilleros, including Gaspar, needed real military training. In mid-1978, 16 of them were sent to study for three months at a special training camp in Cuba. Of the three main courses of study one could choose—weapons use, strategy, and guerrilla technique—Gaspar chose the first. Perhaps he was thinking of the fiasco of the ill-placed machine gun in the Rivas assault. He also decided to specialize in the use of explosives.

The course was rigorous: 10 hours a day in the field, and at other times, long political discussions. The Cubans offered materiel and instructors, but the Nicaraguans needed no help when the time came to analyze political and social questions.

The 16 Nicaraguans created an atmosphere of camaraderie and high spirits. Padre Manuel says Gaspar was a master joke-teller and loved ironic put-downs. But the one subject on which he would tolerate no comic subversion was religion. When other compañeros mocked belief "because faith hasn't succeeded in overthrowing Somoza," Gaspar exploded: "Go to hell, idiots! What I'm fighting for is to bring the people revolution *and* religion. All you want is to bring them revolution. Which is why you'll stumble. You've got to *believe* if you want this revolution to work."

❖

En el seno de las olas	In the breast of the waves
duermes tú.	you sleep.

Y debajo de las copas	And beneath the crowns
de los árboles floridos	of flowering trees
duermes tú.	you sleep.

Y en los rincones perdidos	And in the hidden corners
de las cumbres más hermosas	of the most lovely mountaintops
duermes tú.	you sleep.

| Tú estás en todas las cosas. | You are in all things. |

❖

By August, Gaspar had become one of the Chiefs of Staff of the Southern Front. He was known as an excellent drill instructor, especially when it came to training in weapons use. But above all he was respected as a group leader, a brilliant teacher of the young recruits, who by now were joining the rebels in greater and greater numbers. Most of the muchachos were uneducated campesinos who had enlisted for personal rather than well-reasoned ideological reasons—a sister raped by the Guardia, a father robbed of his land, a brother tortured, a mother dead for lack of expensive medical treatment. Gaspar's expertise was in showing them the links between, say, what happened to one youngster's family, and what was happening to Nicaragua as a whole. While he did tell them about Sandino, about the extent and types of somocista repression, about materialism and idealism, he never harangued or preached at them. His method was frequently Socratic, with the members of the group moving communally toward the recognition of political truths. By hearing themselves and others describe conditions back home, the young recruits came to see who and what they were fighting for and why.

❖

Recordá tus amistades	Remember your friends,
compañero:	compañero:
los perros flacos	the skinny dogs
los perros callejeros	the strays
los que apalean los amos	those their masters beat
los que hurgan basureros	those who poke about in garbage
los que no tienen perrera	those who have no doghouse

los que matan los camiones
en todas las carreteras
los que no tienen derecho
a educarse en las escuelas.

Tú y yo vamos a liberarles
no olvides, guerrillero.

Recordá tus enemigos
compañero:
los perros gordos
los que devoran comida
como cerdos
los que muerden las ovejas
los que van con los negreros
los perros de señorita
los que van al peluquero
los que pasan dormidos
los que muerden a la gente
y los que llaman falderos.

Tú y yo vamos a amarrarlos,
no olvides, guerrillero.

EL ENEMIGO

Eran plagas inmensas de zancudos
 aulladores,
aullaban como perros
y parecían murciélagos
volando.
En el hocico
no tenían nariz ni boca
ni nada animal ni humano.
Eran un inmenso pico
de hierro
largo, recio y afilado.

those run down by trucks
on every roadway
those with no right
to go to school and learn.

Don't forget, we're going to free
 them,
you and I, guerrillero.

Remember your enemies,
compañero:
the fat dogs
who gobble up food
like pigs
those who bite the sheep
those who run with slave traders
the Ladies' Dogs
who go to the hairdresser
those who go by half-asleep
those who bite folks
those they call lapdogs.

Don't forget, we'll tie them up
 tight,
you and I, guerrillero.

THE ENEMY

There was a great plague of
 howling mosquitos,
they howled like dogs,
they were like bats
flying.
On their snouts
they had neither nose nor mouth
they were neither animal nor
 human
there was only an immense beak
of steel
long, cruel, sharpened to a point.

Vivían a expensas de todos:	They lived at the expense of
eran los parásitos.	everyone else:
	they were parasites.
Buscaban la oscuridad,	They sought out darkness,
el silencio y la ignorancia.	silence, ignorance.
Para actuar	To do their work
huían de la luz	they fled from the light
y la verdad.	and from the truth.

❖

For the most part the compañeros loved and respected Gaspar, but there was a side to his character that surprised some of them—his strict (some would say inflexible) adherence to military discipline. On one occasion he discovered that a group of raw recruits was planning to desert, with their weapons, to loot and pillage communities along the border. "His decision," says Padre Manuel, "is categorical. They must be shot. There is no possible excuse. The existence of *orejas* [spies and informers] who continually desert the Frente and thus create practically insoluble problems, has forced them to decide that any spy discovered among the guerrilleros, once his guilt has been established in an open trial, must go before a firing squad. Gaspar feels that while the situation of the potential deserters isn't exactly the same, the results could be similar. And so he orders that they be shot. Only the timely intervention of Edén Pastora saves these poor souls, who had probably assumed that joining the Frente and doing some freelance looting were practically the same thing. Gaspar, however, resists:

"'It's that they'll make us look bad in the eyes of the world.'

"But finally he accedes to Pastora's plea, and the future bandits are merely expelled from the group."

This intransigent, unforgiving streak in Gaspar can be partly explained by the totality of his commitment to be a guerrillero and a good commanding officer: once in uniform, he will not act the part of the merciful priest; he will be all cool military clarity and decisiveness. But the incident recounted above also brings to our minds others moments in Gaspar's life characterized by an absolutist and inflexible option for violence: he throws a "drunken" woman (planted in his room by the Guardia) bodily into the street; he wants to blow Somoza sky high right in San Juan; in at least two poems he says it's better the campesinos should die than live as they do, and in another he predicts "the end of things." And then there is his excessive, death-defying eagerness in combat. There is, in short, a link in Gaspar's character between unquestioning discipline, a willingness that he and others should suffer, and what can only be called an apocalyptic view of pain and death as purifying necessities.

Of course, on a conscious level he sees it simply as a matter of unflinching justice:

La justicia está en la ley;	Justice resides in the law;
y no la puede exigir	and no one can demand it
—al Presidente o al Rey—	—from President or King—
quien no la sabe cumplir.	who's not ready to carry it out himself.

Is this call for tough-minded action mere hollow macho posturing in a difficult situation? I think not. It is entirely consistent with the exigencies of Gaspar's unshakeable and often impatient moral conviction, with the anguished severity that ruled his soul. He will not expect of others what he is unwilling to undergo himself; but others must also measure up to his stringent standards. Otherwise, the world belongs to chaos.

Gaspar was always surrounded by intense young recruits: "Tell us everything you learned in Cuba. Everything." He did his best, again and again. But life in the mountains was not entirely military. Gaspar found time to organize literacy classes for the campesinos who had joined up. Many came out of the guerrilla knowing for the first time how to read and write.

Health problems caused by poor sanitation and nutrition were a constant. The campesinos mostly ate canned food, but bad water led to dysentery. They bathed as frequently as they could, and when this happened, a sort of taboo took over: there were both male and female fighters in Gaspar's unit, and yet they bathed together, naked, without any disruptive incidents. It was a sign of the deep respect and interdependency they felt for one another that the guerrilleros and guerrilleras were able to transcend the sexism and sense of "shame" they'd been raised with.

The men and the women ate, worked, trained, and fought alongside one another, but as Padre Manuel points out, the women's rate of failure was much lower than that of the men. "One could say without fear of error that there was not a single desertion among the women. Some of them left camp for reasons of illness, but always unwillingly. In contrast, there

95

were many untrustworthy men. There were boys who simply couldn't deal with the hardships of life in the mountains and were forced to return home."

Many romances developed in the mountains, and more than a few marriages, which always included the couple's passing under a double file of raised rifles at the conclusion of the ceremony; when the newlyweds reached the end of the "tunnel," all the rifles were fired at once. Padre Ernesto Cardenal, who passed through the encampments of the Southern Front from time to time, officiated at many of these marriages. Gaspar, who went out of his way not to call attention to the fact that he was a priest (Felipe Peña of Solentiname, for instance, learned his commander was a priest only after Gaspar's death), was reluctant to marry couples in his own unit, but on several occasions he was prevailed upon to do so. Some women resented his stubbornness on this point, but others found in Gaspar a useful confidant and friend.

En mi futuro concreto,	In the future as I see it
los hombres vivirán	men will live
como los geranios	like geraniums
de perfume fuerte	with strong scent
y umbelas rojas	and red petals
y las mujeres	and women
como amapolas	like prolific
fecundas.	poppies.
Amapolas y geranios	Poppies and geraniums
darán su fruto	will bear fruit
donde el viento común	where the all-sharing wind
quiera llevarlos.	wants to carry them.

❖

Among the best indicators of Gaspar's state of mind during the final year of his life are two letters written to his brother, Silverio:

"Dear Silverio:

"Just imagine—I've swiped your name, and the letters I send in Central America I sign as though they were from you.

"My own name is so 'burned' that whoever gets a letter from me gets killed. So for the time being, please don't come to Nicaragua, because you'll force me to change my name once again, which will cause no end of confusion.

"I have publicly entered the guerrilla. For four years I have been a secret militant, but when I was discovered, we decided to take full advantage of the opportunity and score big political points in our struggle to overthrow this filthy Somoza dictatorship.

"I've joined up because there is no smoother, clearer course to take. If only we didn't have to risk our lives at every step! If only we didn't have to execute anyone! But the ambition of tyrants is so absolute that they prefer to die rather than simply skip the country with their millions. All too human.

"I suppose my joining up will also 'burn' me in the eyes of our foot-dragging, opportunist Church. I don't worry about it, because what I do I do out of conscience, fulfilling a sacred duty, thinking less of the consequences than of the serious motives that impel me to act, and of the results we hope to obtain.

"Silverio, the Church will respect me only after I've been killed. In the meantime, let them say what they will.

"They're used to being armchair politicians and strict judges of well-set tables and cushy jobs. The step I've taken upsets them and they turn nasty because what I've done rebukes their easy life and their lack of commitment. If they approved of what I've done, they'd have to do the same, and for that they lack the courage.

"You at least respect my commitment.

"I have no personal ambitions. If we gain power, I'll retire to some humble village and be a humble priest. Or perhaps I'll go somewhere else and fight for a better world. I might, I just might.

"I only want to be true to myself and to the commitment which my entire being requires of me. This is very demanding.

"Greeting to my friends.

"For you, a big hug."

The second is addressed from "Somewhere in Nicaragua, General Garrison of the Mountains":

"Dear Silve: As you see, as time passes I become more diligent. In the past, what an effort it was to wring a letter to you out of me, and now I do it every month like a faithful child writing home to his parents.

97

"I do so because the anxiety you must be feeling about my decision pains me.

"Look: I'm in good shape and I'm content. That's first of all. The second thing is that despite the fact that I'm waging war, I'm at peace with myself and I feel happy. The third thing is that there is nothing so worthwhile as giving your life for the liberation of a people. The fourth is, that's what Nicaragua needs now, not sermons. Fifth, that lots of people think as I do but they're afraid, and so do nothing. Sixth, that God wants the liberation of everyone, and all through history He has brought men and opportunities together to accomplish what is destined to be. Seventh, that when we finish our work, I'll simply go on being a priest in some humble town. Eighth, that if another opportunity like the one here in Nicaragua presented itself to me, I'd do the same thing. Ninth, one should use one's membership in a Community as a way of serving people, and not let it be an excuse for inaction when it seems not to fit a concrete situation. What I mean is, when you have a broken toilet, you don't call a doctor, you call a plumber. What Nicaragua needs now is plumbers, because her inner workings are screwed up. Tenth, if we had more people who were committed, this whole thing would end in a couple of days, without a drop of blood spilled. But as it is, it'll go on and on. . . .

"I think the step I've taken has great political importance. It's already had a substantial impact on the country, and several other priests have joined up. And there are two more, that I know of, who will ring the bell any minute now.

"No one's attacking me for the time being. The institutional Church is opportunist and is afraid to come out against us, in case we win. Afterwards they'll come along saying they had an influence on this or that, that they always agreed with us, and why don't we try such and such, etc. What they don't realize is that I will have no influence whatsoever, because when we win I'm going to drop out of sight.

"As a priest I have an obligation to step forward and show my people the way. And in a situation as desperate as the one in which our people are living today, what are needed are men who will stand up against evil. By bearing witness in this struggle I will encourage many others, you can be sure.

"My Community, the Sacred Heart Missionaries, is behaving itself according to what it is—a brotherhood with very clear ideas, and hearts full of love. I spoke to you about this in Spain. So, brother, I feel content, united with all of them, loving them like brothers. Do you see? It's a community which serves a purpose in a different situation, but not in Nicaragua.

"But when Nicaragua is free, then the Sacred Heart Missionaries could come to help build a new revolutionary society. Or they could go to other countries to plant the active seeds of liberty, which will impel people on to ever greater common achievements. And I'll be with them.

"Oh well, I can't explain everything I think in a few lines, but you get the drift.

"All right, brother. Take care of yourself, and may generosity always be at your side. Don't tie yourself down to any community if it's suffocating you, but don't run away from a community out of egoism.

"An enormous hug. Cheers!

"GASPAR"

8

In August, the Terceristas, led by the surviving Ortega brothers Daniel and Humberto, Edén Pastora, and the highest-ranking woman in the FSLN, Dora María Téllez, decided the time had come for a dramatic action to galvanize public support for the Frente and to show Somoza that his regime was vulnerable even in the capital. Thus was born "Operación Chanchera"—Operation Pigpen.

Shortly after noon on August 23, what looked like a standard green military truck pulled up in front of the National Palace where the Chamber of Deputies debated the new budget. Dressed in the uniforms of the Infantry Basic Training School, 25 Sandinistas marched up the steps, into the lobby of the palace, and announced the arrival of President Somoza. "Stand back," barked Pastora. "The Chief is coming." They walked briskly through the building, disarming guards at each checkpoint, and right into the Blue Room where the Chamber of Deputies was in session. Before the lawmakers had time to recognize him, Pastora shouted, "Everyone on the floor! This is the Guardia!" Most deputies thought it was a coup, and meekly complied. There was one brief skirmish with a passing Guardia patrol, and then the building was sealed off from within. Counting deputies, bureaucrats, reporters, and ordinary citizens, there were almost 2,000 hostages.

Over the next two days, Dora María Téllez, using the Catholic bishops as mediators, wrung a series of stunning concessions from Somoza, including an end to sniping and counterattacks on the palace, a ransom of half a million dollars, publication of an FSLN manifesto, freeing of political prisoners from jails around the country, as well as free passage out of Nicaragua for the assault team, the 60 or so newly released prisoners, and a handful of hostages. On August 25, packed into buses, the jubilant Sandinistas made their way through the streets of Managua where thousands of people had turned out to cheer them, out to the airport, and from there to Panama. Somoza and the Guardia had been humiliated. The Sandinistas were overnight heroes.

❖

FSLN

Somos guaria tropical
recia
delicada
pura.

Somos la Flor Nacional
de Nicaragua.

Somos la cara final
exacta
justa
completa.

Somos la hora cabal
de Nicaragua

Somos la liberación
sola
única
total.

Somos la revolución
de Nicaragua.

FSLN

We are the tropical orchid
strong
delicate
pure.

We are the National Flower
of Nicaragua.

We are the final look of things:
exact
just
complete.

We are Nicaragua's finest hour
come round at last.

We are liberation
the one and only
unique
total.

We are Nicaragua's
revolution.

❖

The popular uprising after the capture of the National Palace spread like wildfire. Spontaneous anti-Somoza demonstrations broke out in various cities; but they were brutally suppressed, which added to public outrage. The Guardia was kept busy here today, there tomorrow, a frenetic disarray that left a clear opportunity for the Frente. The Southern Front command used the month of September to infiltrate forces from Costa Rica well into Nicaragua—as far north as the area around San Juan del Sur and Rivas. The idea was to seize key points and declare everything south of Rivas a "free zone." The first attack was on a small outpost called Sotacaballo. As in earlier actions, Gaspar pushed ahead eagerly, impulsively, and was the first to enter the village. And as before, Pastora had to restrain him: "Easy, Gaspar! We can't afford to lose you."

But after the raid on Sotacaballo, logistics problems and Guardia counterpressure made it clear they were in too deep. Pastora gave the order to head back toward the border. During their slow retreat they were detected by the Air Force, which tried to strafe and bomb them. They managed to avoid casualties, but they were tired and hungry.

They came across a farmhouse. In it were some women, children, and old people. They were hungry, too. Gaspar went to a nearby farmer and bought a pig, which they roasted and shared with the inhabitants of the house. Everyone—guerrilleros and campesinos alike—relaxed. There were jokes, songs, stories. Someone produced some hidden coffee. Late in the afternoon, the column said goodbye and headed south. But after an hour or so of marching, Gaspar stopped and said to Chema Guadamuz from San Juan, "Hey, kid. You hungry? I am. Let's go back and get some more of that pig."

They decided to send Germán Pomares back to the farm to get some more of the roast pig. After a while they heard the sound of bombs. Then Pomares returned, pale and angry. The Air Force had flattened the house, bombed it to a pile of smoking rubble. Everyone was dead—the women, the children, the old folks. Everyone.

Now the retreat was sped up; it was raining, the streams swollen; they paused only to freeze in place when a plane swooped by. The Air Force was dropping bombs at random throughout the zone. Despite their fancy hardware, Somoza's men were getting nervous.

❖

Miraba el agua pasar	I watched the water move
mansamente por la tierra	softly across the earth
y la quise comparar	and I wanted to compare it
con el agua de la sierra.	with the water in the mountains.

El agua de la llanura	The water on the plains
de la vida cuando pasa;	gives life as it goes by;
pero el agua de la altura	but the water up there
es una fuerza que mata.	is a force that kills.
Igual sucede a los hombres:	The same with men:
unos riegan ideales;	some water ideals;
otros, odios y pasiones.	others, hatred and passions.
Las aguas no son iguales.	All waters are not equal.

❖

The guerrilleros reached the convent at La Cruz, where they would rest before heading on to San José, just as the nuns had begun supper with some Costa Rican visitors and a young woman visiting from the United States. By now the guerrilleros had hidden their battle gear and were dressed in civilian clothes. Gaspar thought it best to pass themselves off as seminarists on a short excursion. And so the wise nuns, the unsuspecting visitors, and the slightly droopy-looking "seminarists" broke bread together.

But on the way back to San José, the game of clever disguises backfired. In San Dimas, Gaspar decided to dress himself as a local campesino so as to buy food for the other compañeros; but the tall, white-skinned figure wearing combat boots aroused suspicions immediately. He was questioned by the local police, the rest of the band was seized, they were taken to San José, and the next thing they knew they were on a plane to Panama. Deported.

The young woman from the United States was also back in the capital, and when she saw the TV news coverage of the deportation of the Nicaraguan rebels she was stunned. "I know those boys! They're not guerrillas, they're perfectly nice seminary students. There must be some mistake." It took a while to convince her she was wrong.

In Panama, Gaspar became spokesperson for the new arrivals. Reporters from around the world followed him everywhere. He appeared on TV and gave long interviews in which he spoke confidently of their coming victory, set forth his own reasons for taking up arms, and in an unguarded moment, with his typical bravado, told of the plot to blow up Somoza in the streets of San Juan: "A charge of dynamite under the spot where he had to pass, just like they did to Carrero Blanco in Spain." He also told how a "young teacher" from San Juan had helped him with the plot. Unfortunately, the Managua daily *Novedades* picked up the lead and printed the story about the aborted plot against the President of the Republic, masterminded by "the Communist priest García Laviana, in the pay of international Communism, a turncoat to his vocation, in cahoots with a young teacher in his parish." For anyone who knew San Juan, there could be no question who the teacher was, but by a stroke of luck, Juan Brenes heard about the article in time to drop out of sight before being arrested.

Padre Manuel has talked at length with Chema Guadamuz about this period in Panama. Chema reports that despite the high visibility and good propaganda value of the Sandinista presence, Gaspar felt out of his element. He who had begun to taste the exhilarations of nonstop action, of direct engagement with somocismo, of commanding forces in the field, found himself oppressed by the inactivity of exile. Gaspar, who had taken tranquilizers during the worst periods of stress in San Juan, now began to drink beer for hours at a time. His companion during these failed attempts to induce oblivion was Chema, who partly "attributes this reaction to the disillusionment Gaspar felt when he learned that some of those who had been deported with him had indicated that they would no longer take part in armed struggle, and would instead return to their homes."

Finally, Gaspar and Alejandro Guevara called a meeting of the deportees. The order was given: they would all return to Costa Rica, but they must do so the slow, secret way—over the mountains, in small groups, being careful to attract the attention of neither Panamanian nor Costa Rican police.

Here's how Chema Guadamuz completes the story: he decides to disobey orders. It will take months to get back to San José through the mountains. So instead he takes a Panamanian bus to the border, and there boards a Ticabus headed for San José. And yet as he walks down the aisle he recognizes first one, then another guerrillero from his group. They've all had the same idea. But no one gives the slightest wink, nod or smile of recognition. Alejandro, for one, spends the entire trip staring blankly out the window. . . .

❖

It is worth our while to stand back from the flow of our narrative at this point to examine Gaspar the poet in 1978. In one sense, it is remarkable he found time as a guerrilla commander to write at all. But many who knew him say he would periodically go off by himself, prop himself against a tree, and write in his notebook. If asked what he was writing, he would simply not answer. But we are lucky he took the time to record the inner changes he was going through and the preoccupations that were central to his life at this period.

Aside from the overtly political focus of poems like "FSLN," two main currents flow through Gaspar's poetry during this final year of his life. One is symbolic, darkly allegorical, sometimes dreamlike, mixing ecstasy with uneasiness. In this mode he sometimes feels himself to be a natural force, a part of nature itself, even some physical object.

In one poem he is a ship making its way through a sea whose rich and sensuous promise is somehow overshadowed:

Enmarada en mil perfumes
iba el alma,
inundando mi desierto
de bienestar y fragrancia.

Sailing out into a thousand
        perfumes
went the soul,
flooding my desert
with fragrance and well being.

Dormido con mi presente
iba en calma
navegando mi velero
mecido por la esperanza.

Asleep in my present life
my boat sailed
calmly on,
rocked by waves of hope.

Aunque pesaba en mi vida
toda una ancla,
yo no notaba su hierro
sobre las alas del alma.

Though a huge anchor
was weighing down my life,
I did not feel its iron bulk
on the wings of my soul.

In another, what seems to be an allusion to slain comrades takes as its vehicle the image of boats who have left early, only to perish without him; he longs to join them:

Los barcos que partieron de mi
        playa
se perdieron confundidos en el
        mar.
¡Cómo quisiera perseguir su estela,
alcanzarles y ver el nuevo rumbo
de mi ser, con la nueva
        perspectiva!

The boats that left from my
        beach
have all been lost at sea.
How I long to follow their wake,
join them and see the new
        direction
of my being, its new perspective!

In the following poem, the natural, almost erotic images of self-hood shift with dizzying rapidity, as though the poet—and his friend or friends—could not bear to remain fixed in a single identity:

Soy
vivero de amapolas,
arado de eriales,
río profundo.

I am
hotbed of poppies,
plow to untilled lands,
deep river.

Soy
marea inexorable
volcán violento,
llama viva.

I am
inexorable tide,
violent volcano,
living flame.

Somos
mar con mar junto a la playa,
mezcla de espuma con espuma,
ola con ola.

We are
sea against sea near the shore,
foam mixed with foam,
wave with wave.

Or in a similar vein of protean personal allegory:

Soy como el buen estiércol,
sembrado de suciedad
en campos yermos.

I'm like good manure
scattered in all its filth
over barren fields.

Arma de verdad
sin balas de justicia.

Weapon of truth
without bullets of justice.

Ola que se derrama
junto a la orilla.

Wave that spills itself
nearing the shore.

Ola de playa.

Surf.

And again, in what looks like a mere fragment, more fusion (maybe confusion) of the self with the world:

. . . siento mi ser
crecer,
semi-hombre,
semi-piedra,
como tejido de hiedra
que va por el mundo
sin nombre
y sin rumbo.

. . . I feel my being
grow:
half man
half stone
like a mat of ivy
that spreads through the world
without name
without direction.

The images of the sea and boats are recurrent, as in this Dantean before-and-after dream:

Rumbo a la tierra perenne,	As I near the deathless land,
marinero,	sailor,
quiero mirar en la orilla	I want to see on the shore
la solemne	the imposing
maravilla	spectacle
de un gigante prisionero.	of an imprisoned giant.
Miré al gigante encerrado	I saw him, the giant
en la arena;	in chains on the sand;
y le escuché un bramido	and I heard his roar,
fatigado,	weary,
afligido,	pained,
recusando su condena.	protesting his punishment.

The other current in these late poems is less rhetorical and displaced, more direct. The poems tend to be rawer, less worked over, more dashed-off, but more haunted. He foresees his death and is filled with anxiety, as much over the consequences and aftermath of his dying as over the experience itself.

Yo tengo una señal	There is a sign
de muerte	of death
clavada en la laringe	stuck in my windpipe
como un puñal	like a stab
de fiebre . . .	of fever . . .
Es la muerte, es la muerte	It's death, it's death
en mi garganta . . .	in my throat . . .
Y me espanta	And it terrifies me
pensar	to think
que un día me hará callar.	one day it will silence me.

The premonitory anguish takes several forms. In one poem he regrets not being able to see the fruits of his labors. (The Camilo in this poem probably refers to the Colombian guerrillero-priest Camilo Torres, although it may refer to Camilo Ortega.)

¡Qué duro es morir	How hard it is to die
sin ver el triunfo!	without seeing the Triumph!
Creo que lo mismo	I suppose

sintió Cristo	Christ must have felt the same
y Camilo	and Camilo
y Che Guevara.	and Che Guevara.

Any consolation in dying is treated either perfunctorily—

A morir, a morir,	Toward death, toward death,
guerrillero,	guerrillero,
que para subir	because to rise
al cielo,	to heaven,
hay que morir	you've got to die
primero.	first.

—or with a touch of irony that recalls Gaspar's letter to his brother ("The Church will respect me only after I've been killed."). The following poem takes its ruling metaphor from "oro verde," the name of a premium grade of coffee bean. Here it represents some glittering, elusive goal sought by the guerrilleros:

Oro verde	Green gold
oro verde	green gold
no se compra con dinero	simply can't be bought with
no es del mundo el oro verde	money
es del cielo.	it isn't of this world, green gold
	it's from heaven.

Oro verde	Green gold
oro verde	green gold
va buscando el guerrillero	is what the guerrillero seeks
yo también busco oro verde	I seek it too, that green gold
compañero.	compañero.

Oro verde	Green gold
oro verde	green gold
cuando ya nos vean muertos	when at last they see us dead
nos darán el oro verde	then they'll give us green gold
guerrilleros.	guerrilleros.

But just as in the poem printed above he yearns to follow the wake of the departed boats, so in his blunter mode, he voices a desperate wish to suffer and even die alongside his beloved campesinos:

¡Escuchadme, perros flacos:	Listen, strays and mongrels:
escuchad mi testamento!:	Here is my will:
Yo quiero estar con vosotros,	I want to be with you,
mis hermanos,	my brothers,
hasta el último momento . . .	until the bitter end . . .
No te quiero, perro gordo,	I don't love you, fat dog,
porque devoras el oro	because you gobble gold
como un cerdo,	like a pig
y condenas a mis perros	and condemn my dogs
a que mueran en el lodo.	to die in the mud.
¡Yo quiero morir con ellos!	I want to die with them!

He even feels an urge to stage-manage his own funeral rites, but the impulse is full of a half-submerged, violent rage:

Cuando ganemos la guerra,	When we win the war
no vengáis con pungidos a mi tumba	Don't come full of remorse to my tomb
con rosas y claveles	with roses and carnations
rojos, como mi sangre derramada.	red like my spilled blood.
Os juro que me levantaré	I swear I'll rise up
y os azotaré con ellos.	and whip you with them.
Solo admitiré violetas	I will only allow violets
como mi carne macerada,	just like my battered flesh,
como el dolor de mi madre,	like my mother's grief,
como el hambre campesina	like the hunger
de mi América Latina.	of the campesino
	of my Latin America.

In one fragment he sees all the good he's done undone by unnamed others:

. . . he defendido mi libertad en la vida	I have defended my freedom in this life.
Pero lo tienen todo,	But they have it all
y también quisieran	and they'd like
echar sus garras a mis obras	to get their claws into
cuando muera.	my work when I die.

¡NO!
¡Que mis obras son del pueblo!

NO!
My work belongs to
the people!

And in another he imagines bitterly the hypocrisy of the powerful in the aftermath of his death:

Cuando muera,	When I die
no quiero que sollocen mentiras	I don't want those
las sanguijuelas del pueblo.	bloodsuckers of the people to
No quiero que me lloren	sob lies.
los perros que comen rebaños de	I don't want those dogs
gente.	that eat people's flocks
No quiero que sus lágrimas saladas	weeping for me.
esterilicen mis obras . . .	I don't want their salty tears
	staining my works.
Cuando me mates, perro gordo,	When you kill me, fat dog,
no quiero que me llores como	I don't want you to weep for me
gente;	like people do.
quiero que me ladres.	Just howl.

I think we have to imagine some of what's been quoted above as having been scribbled down in haste during a lull in combat or a break in training. Despite the sketchiness of some of the poems, they are invaluable gauges of Gaspar's mental and spiritual state. We see in these poems themes we are already familiar with: Gaspar's impatience, his impulsiveness, his rebellious anger toward authority, his deeply romantic identification with the natural world and the people around him, his passionately loving nature. But we also see him preparing himself for the end he now sees as inevitable and close at hand. True, he was finally doing what he wanted to do: he had become a man of action, a militant Christian, commanding his own forces in a struggle that would involve the ultimate sacrifice. But there is no question that he felt a profound ambivalence toward that sacrifice. He knew the fulfillment of his destiny was coming, he knew what he was doing was right, but it frightened him all the same. To my mind, this makes Gaspar more human than most martyrs; and it makes his almost boyish, irrepressible bravery all the more admirable.

❖ ❖ ❖ 9

December 1978. Some of the facts are clear, others hazy or disputed:

The guerrilleros of the Southern Front are divided into about 15 groups, each with its own area of operations, its own base camps, and its own commander.

Gaspar is comandante of Base 13. He and his 80 or so compas will control the large, muddy, rain-soaked area between Cárdenas and Orosí on the Big Lake, stretching back inland to the Costa Rican border.

Pastora has overall control of these bases.

Strict orders come down from the High Command:

—No comandante will personally direct any operation; he will only plan it;

—Don't make your presence in your area known to the Guardia; explore the terrain well, get to know its advantages and shortcomings;

—No comandante should allow himself to be taken prisoner; he must employ all means possible to avoid capture;

—All operations must take place under the supervision of the Commander in Chief; and

—For the time being, undertake *no* operations.

Gaspar visits Pastora: A helicopter has been cruising their area for days now, sometimes hovering practically over their heads.

"It would be so easy to shoot down!" says Gaspar.

"No. You're not supposed to give away your position yet," says Pastora.

"It's big, really big."

"You know the orders, Gaspar."

"But it's fat, really huge and fat. It would be so easy."

"No. Not yet."

Gaspar shakes his head. "Oh well. . . . But every time it goes overhead, my mouth waters."

December 3: The following incident is reported: a small group of guerrilleros, apparently from Gaspar's unit, have attacked a hacienda just over the Costa Rican border, on the mistaken assumption that Guardia were present. In fact, the hacienda belongs to a man who has been collaborating with the Frente. The owner is outraged and demands justice. One witness says he saw Gaspar directing the attack. The Southern Front Command decides Gaspar must be summoned to answer for the attack, and possibly pay damages.

But Gaspar is hard to locate. He is not at the base camp. Instead he is commanding a squad of five men on a probing operation to reconnoitre another hacienda, called Sábalos, partly owned by Somoza's sister Lilián. Of course, Gaspar shouldn't be leading this mission himself; it is directly contrary to orders. But as Padre Manuel puts it, "his restless nature won't let him sit still."

When they arrive at the hacienda, there are no Guardia to be found, but some of the workers recognize the squad's commander:

"It's Padre Gaspar!"

The guerrilleros leave. Half an hour later a patrol of 60 Guardia arrives, looking for rebels.

December 10: Pastora sends Estrella as a second messenger to Gaspar: a meeting must be held to clear up this business about the attack on the Costa Rican hacienda, and to solidify plans for upcoming operations all along the border area. Estrella also carries this pointed repetition of original orders: comandantes should direct operations, not take part themselves. But again, Gaspar is nowhere to be found. He has learned that the Guardia detachment they were looking for at Hacienda Sábalos is in fact now in the vicinity of another hacienda, El Disparate, sometimes also known as El Infierno. Gaspar has taken 30 men and has gone to confront the Guardia. Estrella is unable to deliver her message.

A new rumor reaches Gaspar: the Guardia may actually be at a hacienda called Santa Helena. He changes orders: they will head for Santa Helena instead of El Disparate. The march is agony: rain-swollen rivers, mud, swamps, darkness, mosquitos. When they finally arrive, the hacienda looks quiet, but they keep their distance and watch for several hours: it may be an ambush. At last, when no signs of the Guardia appear, they take the main house. The farm workers tell them the Guardia patrol is at El Disparate.

Gaspar's men are muddy, cold, wet, and exhausted. He decides to let them rest at Santa Helena. He will send ahead the young man who has been serving as their guide; he will return from El Disparate with exact information about the Guardia. . . .

It is at this point in the story that different versions begin to conflict with each other. One version, popular in San Juan, has it that the guide was named "La Cucaracha," that he was from Tola and had recently joined Gaspar's unit as a guerrillero; that his subsequent treachery was typical of the backward morals of the toleños, some of whom were looking for a way to betray Gaspar; that La Cucaracha was later captured and held in the Ministry of Agriculture building in Rivas, or perhaps it was a boat in San Juan harbor. . . .

Padre Manuel says the guide was from the Orosí/Cárdenas region, a young man named Justo Elías Pérez, a noncombatant, someone Gaspar barely knew. . . .

In any case, all who tell this story agree: Gaspar makes a fatal mistake at Hacienda Santa Helena. The guide, whatever his name or provenance, agrees to reconnoiter El Disparate, but asks a single favor of Gaspar: his brother works on the farm at El Disparate. If there's going to be a battle, he wants to be able to warn his brother to get himself and his family away before it's too late.

In purely military terms, the correct decision would have been (a) to distrust an untried outsider on a delicate mission requiring courage and commitment, and (b) to forbid him to tell *anyone* about their plans to attack the Guardia. Better yet, now that Gaspar knows the guide has family involved, the obvious move should have been to send someone else to gather the information.

But faced with a young campesino who has served them well (at least for the past couple of days) and who asks only that his family be spared the crossfire, Gaspar becomes once again his old empathetic priestly self:

of course the guide can warn his brother. "Just tell your brother to tell the boss your uncle in Jinotepe is gravely ill and he has to visit him before he dies."

And so off goes the guide toward El Disparate. "If he can pull this off and make it back alive, we ought to build him a monument," jokes Alejandro.

But the situation at the farm is more complicated than Gaspar realizes. The guide's brother is married to the daughter of the owner of the farm. Apparently, the guide warns his brother, his brother tells the wife, the wife tells her father, and the father tells the Guardia, who instantly grill the guide: Where are the rebels? How many are there? What are their plans?

All this takes time. When the guide doesn't return, Gaspar gets suspicious. He should be back by now. Meanwhile, they are sitting ducks. Gaspar decides to act: they head for El Disparate, not on the road, but through the backwoods, to confront the enemy—assuming they're there.

The Guardia meanwhile heads for Santa Helena, but via the road.

Gaspar and his men arrive at El Disparate at midnight. They are soaked to the skin and dead tired. From the top of a low hill they can make out the house, 800 meters away, on the other side of the Río Mena. Gaspar divides his men into three groups: Pichardo's squad will cross the river and come at the house from the rear, Jerónimo's will situate themselves on an adjacent hill, and Gaspar's will control the key observation point. At six in the morning, first light, Gaspar will begin the attack. The fire from the two hills will distract the Guardia so that Pichardo's group can move in for an assault from behind.

Meanwhile the Guardia, finding no one at Santa Helena, are on their way back to El Disparate. The road passes alongside the two hills where the guerrilleros are hidden by nothing more than tall grass. Gaspar and his men are ready for an attack on the house; they are not, however, ready for an ambush from the Guardia.

At six, the guide and the forward unit of the Guardia come into view. The rebels crouch down in the grass. Then one of Gaspar's men (it has never been determined who) says: "Look! There goes the guide!"

The Guardia column stops. An officer shouts, "Who goes there?" When there is no answer, he orders his men to open fire on Gaspar's hill. The rebels return fire. Bullets fly in all directions, one catches Gaspar in the thigh.

"Ay, Mamita! They got me!"

He stands up, his rifle blazing.

A burst of fire from the Guardia rakes his right side from top to bottom. He falls dead into a low trench behind him, next to the body of "Tonino" Arroyo who has also been cut down.

Steady fire from Jerónimo's men allows the rest of Gaspar's group to retreat. Pichardo, who at first assumed the gunfire was directed at the house, now sees his compañeros fleeing across the river and realizes what is happening. He orders his own men to retreat to the river.

"Santiago," a young man from Estelí, freezes in mid-river. He doesn't know how to swim. He calls out to his friends for help, in vain. He is captured by the Guardia. (He will later be brutally tortured, then shot.) No one knows yet that Gaspar has fallen.

When the rest of the rebels have crossed the river and melted into the mists of the early morning, the Guardia finds the bodies. The commanding officer gives the *coup de grace* to Gaspar, a single shot at close range that passes through the top of the skull and shatters his jaw.

It is still raining.

Later that day, Judge Jamil Herrera got a call from the Guardia: he was needed in Orosí to identify some bodies. Standard procedure: identification, certificates of death, the usual thing. Jamil had refused that sort of request as frequently as he could, fearing a trap to finger him as a Sandinista. Only days before, he had declined to identify some bodies being flown to Rivas; the helicopter as it turned out had crashed and burned on landing. But this time the Guardia was insistent. Jamil checked with his brother Hebert, who told him there were now reports trickling in that Gaspar García Laviana had fallen in action somewhere on the Southern Front. And so Jamil agreed. Among those in the helicopter that made the half-hour flight to El Disparate were Colonel Ebertz and Gaspar's old enemy, Dr. Caldera.

When they reached the spot where the bodies were still stretched out on the ground, Jamil immediately recognized not only Gaspar, but also his old schoolboy chum Luis "Tonino" Arroyo. Jamil said nothing, showed nothing.

"Is it Gaspar?" asked Ebertz.

"I can't tell."

"What do you mean you can't tell, when he's a close friend of you and your brother?"

117

"Of me? He said mass in my hometown, but I had nothing to do with him."

"But you were with him in Tola and San Juan. I'll ask you again: do you recognize him?"

"I don't know who this is. My job is to confirm if he's dead or not. That I confirm. Nothing else."

Ten minutes later the helicopter came back with the body of Santiago. Dr. Caldera, who had given a cursory glance at the bodies, was chatting with the Guardia.

Jamil said to Ebertz: "We ought to take them to Rivas. With the helicopter it would be easy."

And the reply: "We don't want any problems or demonstrations. It's better if we leave them here. Let the dogs eat them."

On the ground was a black beret. Jamil could see powder burns on Gaspar's head and the gaping hole in his cheek. But there were no signs of torture, which was some relief.

When no one was paying attention, Jamil slipped his hand into Gaspar's shirt pocket, took out some letters, and hid them in his own pocket. When he got back to Rivas he read the letters. They were from a young woman who wanted to join the Frente. In one of the letters, she mentioned her contact—Madelina Flores, Gaspar's occasional secretary, who is responsible for the survival, in typed form, of much of Gaspar's early and middle poetry. Jamil's furtive move to take the letters from Gaspar's body almost certainly saved Madelina's life.

Word of Gaspar's death spread quickly, in Nicaragua and beyond. Estrella's parents, Olga and Napoleón García, were walking on the beach in the Costa Rican town they had fled to after the Guardia had burned down their house in Peñas Blancas, as a punishment for helping the Sandinistas. Toward them came a young man with a transistor radio clapped to his ear. He suddenly cried out as though in pain and threw the radio into the sand. Tears were streaming down his face.

"What is it, son?"

"They've killed Padre Gaspar."

Later that day the Frente's clandestine station Radio Sandino confirmed the rumor.

State-controlled TV in Nicaragua that night showed the goriest possible photo of Gaspar's body, with the head twisted to show the huge black hole cause by a bullet fired at point blank range. The image remained on the screen for a full five minutes.

The front page of *Novedades* was devoted entirely to the "Guardia victory" at El Disparate, also known as El Infierno. The headline read: COMMUNIST PRIEST DIES IN "THE INFERNO."

At the hacienda near Orosí, the Guardia buried Gaspar, Tonino, and Santiago in shallow graves. "There are some," says Padre Manuel, "who say they were buried with their mouths open or with parts of their bodies above ground. This is not true. The reality is that they were buried at no very great depth. Suspecting that the Sandinistas might look high and low in the area to discover the bodies and make away with them, special guards were placed at the gravesite. Three days later, a small group of guerrilleros managed to creep up on the graves and study their placement so that the bodies might be spirited away at some later date. Once the High Command was informed, the necessary steps were taken to prepare to retrieve the bodies. But for the time being, given the vigilance of the Guardia, there was nothing to do but to wait. . . ."

When the Sacred Heart Missionaries in Nicaragua heard of Gaspar's death, they immediately informed the Regional Superior, Padre Josep Maria, in Guatemala, and then set about to recover the body of their brother, to give him a decent burial. When they asked Colonel Ebertz in Rivas, he told them it was out of his hands and suggested they speak to his superiors at the Guardia headquarters in Managua. Officials from the Spanish Embassy joined the missionaries' efforts to retrieve the body, but the Guardia Office of Public Relations only gave them more run-around: "There's nothing we can do. It's a question for the Ministry of the Exterior. Or the Ministry of Health." But when inquiries were directed to these ministries, the result was the same.

Meanwhile, Padre Josep Maria had arrived in Nicaragua. He asked the Papal Nuncio to do what he could; as it happened, the Nuncio had already asked Somoza, in person, to give them the body, to which Somoza had replied: "There's a lot of dead people out there. We can't spend our days digging up bodies."

News of Gaspar's death reached Tola during the celebration surrounding the Feast of the Virgin of Guadalupe, the very holiday whose secular manifestations Regalado had tried to suppress. As you remember, it was Gaspar himself who had later allowed the traditional noisy carnival atmosphere to continue side by side with the religious observances. A sullen peace had reigned in Tola since then, but the death of their controversial parish priest brought all the latent hostilities to the surface again. The somocistas and others who had resented being preached at by a fervent leftist with undisguised sympathies for liberation movements and campesino rights, took the unexpected turn of events as an occasion for a triumphal celebration of the burden that had been lifted from their lives. Instead of praying in mournful silence for the repose of Gaspar's soul, they took to the streets shouting and singing, urging their hired musicians to strike up ever louder, ever more raucous fanfares.

The gasparistas, many of whose sons, daughters, brothers, and sisters had joined Gaspar "in the mountains," (in Nicaragua, "in the mountains" or "irse en la montaña" means to join the guerrilla movement) were enraged. They confronted the merrymakers in the streets. Shouting matches erupted, with Gaspar's partisans threatening to rip down any decorations not of a strictly religious character. There was pushing and shoving, and despite the arrival of a Guardia patrol (called in by the somocistas), the gasparistas managed to trash a fair portion of the secular banners, festoons, ribbons, and booths set up by the traditionalists.

The divisions in Tola were a microcosm of the animosities that would embitter Nicaraguan society for years to come, even after the triumph of the revolution.

San Juan del Sur was less divided and more ready to grieve openly and unequivocally for its fallen priest. For more than a month after his death, Gaspar was remembered in masses, memorial services, songs, and Gregorian chants, and—although no one knows where they came from— photographs of Gaspar began to appear all over town, on doors and lampposts, on fruit vendors' stalls, and on the trees that line the waterfront boulevard. Below the determined, smiling face were the words:

PADRE GASPAR GARCIA LAVIANA

Sacerdote español de la Congregación de Misioneros del Sagrado Corazón de Jesús, quien por muchos años laboró en la parroquia de San Juan del Sur, Depto. de Rivas. Y que ofrendó su vida por la liberación de Nicaragua, el 11 de Dic. 1978.

PADRE GASPAR GARCIA LAVIANA
Spanish priest of the Congregation of the
Missionaries of the Sacred Heart of Jesus,
who for many years worked in the parish
of San Juan del Sur, Dept. of Rivas.
And who gave his life for the liberation
of Nicaragua, the 11th of December, 1978.

Among the San Juan del Sur commemorations of Gaspar's death, two stand out, one without his body present, and one, almost a year later, with his remains home at last. The first, a Mass for the Dead, was planned Monday, December 18, a week to the day after the fight at El Disparate. Gaspar's bishop, Monsignor López Fitoria, reluctantly agreed to come down from Granada to officiate. "But," he told Padre Josep Maria, "if you want a homily, you'll have to give it yourself. I will have nothing to say."

On the morning of the 18th, the church began to fill up. Vehicles arrived from all over southwestern Nicaragua. The Guardia set up a roadblock at La Virgen and body-searched everyone, including the nuns. And still people streamed into San Juan. The church bell that had enraged the Guardia after the assassination of Pedro Joaquín Chamorro rang slowly and steadily.

At last, when the church could hold no more, Monsignor López Fitoria celebrated the Mass, but throughout the ceremony he was, says Padre Manuel, "dry and distant." He mentioned not a single virtue or good work of Gaspar's; he barely mentioned his name.

But Padre Josep Maria's homily was in a different mode altogether. He denounced the suggestion in *Novedades* that Gaspar had abandoned his priesthood. He stated the consensus of the Sacred Heart order that, when the body was recovered, Gaspar should be buried in San Juan del Sur, near the people he loved so well, and who loved him in return.

Madelina Flores, who had typed clean copies of so many of Gaspar's poems, recorded the homily on a Dictaphone.

". . . I first met Gaspar," said Josep Maria, "exactly 20 years ago, when he began his religious life. When he commenced his novitiate, I had just begun my priestly duties, and my superiors had assigned me to the novitiates' house. During this year of his novitiate, I was Padre Gaspar's confessor. Then, for 16 years, we lost track of each other. But in the last few years, I renewed my contact with him, as his Superior, and by this means I grew acquainted with many of the problems he faced. And when, after this long stretch of time without seeing him, I met him again, I saw once more that accumulation of qualities the Lord had given him, that you here today know so well: a sympathetic man, an open man, generous, with a formidable knack for getting to know people, with a great and giving nature. At times he appeared severe, but at heart he was a man of sentiment, and perhaps for this reason he was also a poet. But these qualities, I say, that I had noticed at the time of his novitiate, had grown and matured. And along with this there was also something we must remember, which is that he chose to serve the Lord as a Missionary of the Sacred Heart, a congregation that has a certain *charisma*—we call *charisma* in its simplest sense whatever unifies a religious group and characterizes its mode of action—among whose principal features is an overwhelming preoccupation with people, especially the most needy. A group that believes firmly in God's love, that believes that if people accept this love in their hearts, our problems can be resolved. That is the mission of our congregation.

"But, brothers and sisters, we know that God's love is not something up there in the clouds. God's love cannot be reduced solely to some cult or other, however good and holy it may be. God's love requires from us a response which shows itself in our love for others, love for our fellow man. I believe I can say with total sincerity that Padre Gaspar lived his vocation as a Missionary of the Sacred Heart with complete intensity. I think you are better judges of this than I, because it is you who felt the force of his efforts, you who witnessed directly the results of his generous giving of himself, above all to those who needed most, by which I mean the campesinos.

"I know that when he arrived in the Americas for the first time and met with a deeply entrenched social situation, it was a deep shock for him, a shock which, in a sense, marked his way of being and acting. And in this sense I believe we can say that Padre Gaspar followed Christ.

"Later, circumstances wrought a change in him, a change which bothered many people, a change which we do not wish to justify here today, but which we need to understand. It is my personal opinion that in this change, right or wrong, Gaspar was motivated precisely by love of his fellow man. This change brought him to see things in a way that profoundly influenced what we would call his conscience. And it's true that this may have brought him to act in ways that, objectively, may not be acceptable. All the same, we must not forget that a person must always act according

123

to what in his conscience he believes is right, even though it may be in a sense wrong.

"Brothers and sisters, I am going to tell you today with complete sincerity, here in public, that for my part I do not accept the path of violence. I don't accept it because it does not seem to me appropriate. On the other hand, I will also tell you that I feel a profound respect for Padre Gaspar as a compañero, and for the courage which brought him to that personal immolation which he felt was right.

"I believe we must all try to see things in this light. Agree with him or not, as you like, but no one can deny that when a person reaches the point where he is ready to sacrifice himself for what he believes is right, for love of his neighbor, he is worthy of respect, even admiration.

"Let me add, on another subject, that I want to clarify in public claims made in certain broadcasts and publications. In fact I want to deny them, because I feel they are slanders, and to slander a person, no matter whom, is always a sin. The slander is that Padre Gaspar abandoned his congregation, abandoned his priesthood, even abandoned the Church.

"Brothers and sisters, let me tell you that is completely false. The 8th of January of this year, a Sunday, I had completed celebrating Holy Mass and upon opening the paper I discovered with great surprise a letter published by Padre Gaspar in which he set forth the reasons for which he made his personal choice. As it happened, the Father General of the Congregation happened to be with us in those days, to preach at one of our retreats. I was at his room, I showed him the letter, he read it, and then we discussed it.

"I said to him: 'It is my intention to travel tomorrow to Nicaragua to see if I can speak to Padre Gaspar. What is his juridical situation, in terms of our rules?' The Father General answered me in the following words, and I quote: 'The Padre has not asked to leave the Congregation. The Congregation respects the personal choices of its members. All the same, if you do catch up with the Padre, tell him from me, the Father General, that the Congregation is going to enforce no sanctions against him.'

"I went. I failed to find Padre Gaspar. But the point is that no matter what, Padre Gaspar died as a member of the Missionaries of the Sacred Heart. . . ."

". . . Brothers and sisters, let me thank you for coming today, and ask you to pray for Padre Gaspar García Laviana."

❖ ❖ ❖ 10

Nineteen seventy-nine brought the Triumph, as broad sectors of Nicaraguan society, from bankers and businesspeople to campesinos and factory workers—and at the last possible moment the Church hierarchy—threw their support behind the Sandinista-led insurrection.

As the Southern Front fell into the hands of the revolutionary forces once and for all, the bodies of Gaspar and the others were disinterred, put into coffins, and moved to the big truck warehouse at the Peñas Blancas border station.

Napoleón García, back from exile, put himself in charge of security and honors for the remains of his old friend Gaspar. Expert artisan that he was, he made a large cross, adorned with seashells and wooden matchsticks, and propped it against the coffin, along with a red and black bandana and a pair of boots that had belonged to Gaspar.

When you visit San Juan, ask Catucha to show you these and other relics, such as the pants Gaspar died in: "It took me forever to get the blood out. I washed and washed. For the longest time the stain simply wouldn't come out."

She keeps these things in a special cabinet in the Casa Cural and spreads them out on a big table for visitors to examine the identification tags she has sewn into the clothes or glued to the cross and the boots.

❖

With the exhilaration and chaos of the post-Triumph period, it was not until mid-September that a move to give Gaspar and his compañeros a proper burial was organized. Padre Josep Maria's successor as Regional Superior, Padre Jaime, came to Nicaragua from Guatemala after receiving word from the new government that the time had come to arrange the burial. But Jaime had walked into the middle of an extremely bitter dispute over who would get Gaspar's body.

Rivas claimed him: Rivas was the departmental seat, the largest town in the area, and Gaspar's center of operations during the CEPA campaign to bring new ideas to the campesinos.

Tola claimed him: Gaspar had been parish priest in Tola during the period of his radical decision to take up arms against Somoza; many guerrilleros had come from Tola, following Gaspar's example; and besides, Tola had constructed a special "Cemetery of the Martyrs," which had already begun to receive the remains of revolutionary heroes.

San Juan claimed him: The people of San Juan had always assumed that if Gaspar died, he would be buried alongside the church that had been his home for so many years; the Sacred Heart Missionaries had stated their preference for San Juan; Gaspar himself had said on more than one occasion, "If I die, bury me in San Juan, facing the sea, so I can see those wonderful sunsets."

The Frente found itself in a bind. How could they decide? They turned to one of the people who knew Gaspar best during his months as a guerrillero: Estrella. She talked with all the parties involved and then made her decision. Padre Manuel recapitulates her reasoning: "Gaspar is by now a symbol for all of Nicaragua. He's not the property of one or another group; he belongs to everyone. Wherever he ends up, the town that has him will be nothing more than custodian of a national hero. And the burial site must be decided on the basis of his characteristics as a national hero. He fought for sandinismo. Who more than all others had followed him into combat? Tola appears to be the town that best answered his call: many of her men and women joined the Frente thanks to Gaspar. Tola's argument thus carries the most weight. What's more, it was in Tola that Gaspar first played a role as a Sandinista, and it was there that he took his first steps toward armed struggle. It was there that he saw clearly for the first time the path he had to take. What's more, Tola has everything prepared."

When the sanjuaneños heard the news, they quickly formed a committee, composed of Emilio Gonzales, José Raúl Muñiz, Lidia Cantillano,

Teodora Granja, Yssy Warren, and others to lobby the Frente to reverse the decision. But it was too late. As Padre Manuel puts it, "unlike the toleños, who are eminently foresighted, sanjuaneños always act at the last minute."

❖

The morning of October 4th, Padre Jaime arrived in Peñas Blancas with a truck to transport the bodies of Gaspar, Tonino, Santiago, and two other compañeros from the region who had fallen during the last months of the struggle. The padre held a service outside the warehouse, attended by Gaspar's brother Silverio, and his sister, Marisa, who had just arrived from Spain, accompanied by a sizeable Spanish delegation, including the mayor of Aviles, and numerous Sandinista officials. After prayers and some speeches, the caravan set out for San Juan.

They arrived at the church at high noon. The heat was withering. The building was packed with sanjuaneños, toleños, and people from the outlying aldeas. The five coffins were placed on the altar, with Gaspar's in the middle, draped with three flags: Spain, Asturias, and the red and black of the FSLN. After the service, a military parade began. The troops surrounding the coffins were meant as much for protection as for honor: the Frente organizers of the funeral had gotten wind of the passions sweeping through San Juan—the grief mixed with outrage, the love for Gaspar mixed with the old rivalrous animus against Tola. There had been rumors that a plot was afoot to steal the body, or substitute another for Gaspar's.

And there had been the episode at the Managua airport when Silverio and Marisa arrived: the San Juan delegation, led by Emilio Gonzales, had spoken with them over the barricade separating public from travellers at Customs. Silverio had at first reiterated his understanding that Gaspar's wish was to be buried in San Juan. But someone from the Frente must have spoken to him, because by the time they had cleared Customs and Immigration, Silverio was saying that it wasn't up to him, and apparently Tola had been chosen by the Frente, and he would accede to their wishes.

In this highly charged atmosphere, the Frente wanted as much dignity and control as possible. The military Guard of Honor stuck close to the coffins.

But in the streets the mood shifted. The people of San Juan began to shout and weep. They were hungry for a more heartfelt, more thorough farewell than they had yet had. They wanted to carry their beloved Gaspar themselves to the outskirts of town and only there yield him up to the

Tola contingent. After hasty negotiations, the Frente organizers decided to let San Juan have its wish. And so the sanjuaneños lifted the five coffins, Gaspar's last, onto their shoulders and began their slow progress through the town.

Everyone wanted to help carry Gaspar. The coffin kept being shifted from shoulder to shoulder. The procession shuffled forward at a snail's pace. People came out of their houses to touch the coffin and add their bodies to the throng. As they approached the port, the women of San Juan, who had been shunted aside up to this point, demanded their right to carry their priest; and so a group of women, one at each corner, bore Gaspar slowly down along the sea road.

The procession through town lasted four hours. At 5 o'clock they arrived at the Texaco station near what is now the Health Clinic, where the other four coffins were waiting, and where Gaspar was to be handed over to the toleños. But the sanjuaneños made no move to relinquish the coffin; they had simply not finished saying goodbye to their priest. A Sandinista guerrillera named María, a Spaniard like Gaspar, spoke to the crowd, urging them to adhere to their agreement, and not do something they would later regret. But the mood was against her. After another hasty conference, the Frente decided to allow the mourners to march another kilometer or so, down the hill, along the river, as far as the bridge, and there—finally—to let Gaspar go.

But what the Sandinista coordinators of the event did not realize is that the road toward Ostional, which also passes the town cemetery, turns off to the right between the filling station and the bridge. When the weeping, shouting throng reached the turn off, which they had taken so many times over the years bearing the coffins of their dead loved-ones, the procession simply plunged off the paved road and headed for the cemetery. "No one decided," says Emilio. "It just happened. No one knew what they'd do with the coffin. All they knew was they didn't want to give him up."

The Sandinistas acted quickly, sending a couple of jeeps around to block the road. Finally, after much argument and more tears, the procession reversed direction and made its way to the bridge.

Even at the bridge they were reluctant to let go. They cried out to Silverio: "Speak! Tell them Gaspar should stay here!"

Silverio, overcome with emotion, whispered, "It's up to the Frente. Whatever they decide."

"But Tola doesn't want him!" cried someone in the crowd.

Silverio wisely saw a compromise. He took from atop the coffin the cross of matchsticks and seashells, the red and black bandana, and Gaspar's boots, and presented them to Emilio, who seemed to be the unspoken leader of the sanjuaneños. In a brief speech, Silverio told the people about how much Gaspar loved San Juan and its people. The crowd grew quiet. He thanked them for their outpouring of affection for his brother. He would never forget it.

The toleños loaded Gaspar on the truck, then drove off down the dirt road called "La Chocolata," the road that Gaspar had driven so many times in the white Renault. "Many sanjuaneños," says Emilio, "kept on walking, down La Chocolata, toward Tola, to be there at the burial. Many. Dozens."

❖

How does one sum up so complex a figure as Gaspar García Laviana? Dare one try?

As a first stab at understanding Gaspar, the psychological approach is clearly inviting: it allows us to deal with details in Gaspar's story that have doubtless troubled the attentive reader.

Gaspar was subjectively radical long before he'd heard of the Sandinistas. He took his Christianity straight and undiluted; he took Christ's challenge literally; the more militant strains in the Gospels were his marching orders. In Nicaragua, he found himself testing the limits of Christianity, seeing how far he could push it, how far he could push himself toward its terrifying goals. This meant trying to discover how much of the pain of others he could experience. His poems about campesinos move from sympathy to desperate identification with them, alive or dead. I have suggested earlier that Spanish Catholicism itself, from Saint Ignatius's *Spiritual Exercises* and the horrors of the Inquisition to the present, has been obsessed with forging links between spirituality and pain. It seems to me that this drive of Gaspar's to get out of his own body (which he tended to neglect or abuse or submit to ordeals) and into the bodies of his long-suffering campesinos, is entangled with unresolved, unconscious, or semiconscious material in his own life. When, for instance, he feels that it is better they should die than go on suffering any longer, the impulse strikes us as being not sadistic/apocalyptic alone; it also sounds masochistic and suicidal. Where this suicidal impulse comes from we can only guess, but my guess is this: Gaspar's agony, which he projected onto—as much as discovered in—the campesinos, came from a horrifying recognition of the parallel, not

129

to say secret identity, between somocismo's casual orgy of brutality and Gaspar's own fascination with pain—pain inflicted and pain suffered. Perhaps the Guardia's appetite for causing pain and death answered a similar impulse in a man who was ready to blow Somoza to bits, kick a half-naked woman into the street, toss a grenade into a house, become an expert in firearms and explosives, and prefer the death of his campesinos (and his own death along with them) to their continued humiliation.

But while Gaspar was a passionate man, he was often searingly aware of his own impulses and how they led him to act. The realization of his own propensity for violence must have been at times intolerable to him. The agony of his choice to become a guerrillero was not merely the result of a philosophical or ethical dilemma. It was an agony born of self-recognition, recognition of his own fallen humanity, of the inextricable interweaving of his authentic impulse toward caritas and a powerful willingness to inflict (and thus participate in) pain.

I think it is not difficult to see a link between inflicting and participating: for a priest to see clearly his own darker, more violent side means, in Gaspar's case, to find a way to punish himself, beginning with seeking out discomfort (the neglect of his body and clothing, the spartan diet, the rigors of guerrilla life) and on to foolhardy risk-taking (striding first into combat in Rivas and Sotacaballo, with Edén Pastora's mother-hen voice at his back like a feeble super-ego: "Not so fast! Watch out! Restrain yourself!"), and on to even greater risk (disobeying orders to avoid combat on the Southern Front and then standing up in the knee-high grass that December morning at El Disparate to face the guns of the Guardia), which we can only describe as a steady, fearless, but compulsive march toward his own death, acceptance of which must have struck him as both self-immolation and self-purification.

The psychological approach has an attractive tidiness as an explanatory mode. But the explanation seems inadequate, or at least incomplete, precisely because it fails to account either for his remarkable achievement as a poet, or for the powerful impact he had on individual people and on the historical destiny of his adopted land.

If we look to the poetry for keys to the secrets of Gaspar's soul we can see certain major recurring preoccupations—love, campesinos, anger, suffering, his compañeros in the guerrilla, his impending death. But these large themes are multifaceted and multivalent, and they tend to be interwoven with one another. He does not speak with a single voice in these poems, but the multiple voices, with their changing emphases, tell a coherent story—partly Gaspar's, and partly Nicaragua's.

As we have seen earlier, the love he feels is occasionally a semi-erotic longing for The Friend who comes in the night (notice that in the line "te sentí toda en el alma" ["All I felt was you in my soul"] "all" is in the feminine); but unlike the drunk declaiming in the street, Gaspar cannot seem to express the burdens of his heart. Once, the love song is directed to God, who is in all things. And in one fragment he seems to be declaring his marriage vows to the rural poor: "The future of my dreams / and yours / for richer or for poorer / is the same, / campesino." At other times, love for the campesinos manifests itself as a compassionate caritas: they are hungry, ignorant, sick, dying. The poet laments their suffering. Sometimes he scolds them for their stubbornness. Frequently, he empathizes with their agony. He suffers José Pérez's death almost as much as does the dying man himself. The poverty of the campesinos is like a whip lashing his flesh, a flame in his bowels. Their misfortune and powerlessness wound him; after a certain point, their poverty and sorrow are his as well.

What strikes us most about the poems of empathetic agony is how physical the imagery of vicarious pain becomes: there are branding irons, bleeding wounds, fiery lashes, spilled blood, battered flesh; there is cancer, hunger, his womb (!) ripped open in the throes of childbirth; there is the threat addressed to the landowners that he will cut his flesh into strips and hang it on their fences until they're forced to flee; there is a generalized threat to scorch the world . . . but with his verses. These supercharged accusations in the early poems against his enemies—the complacent church, the callous landowners, the owners of brothels, the brutal Guardia—seem a bit hysterical, a cry of impotent anger against implacable evils.

But the blind rage and the physical anguish of vicarious suffering are transformed and the masochism is transcended, outgrown, once the decision is made to participate directly in the revolution. Once he's become a combatant, the agonized writhing of the empathetic observer is replaced by the tough, resolute, hopeful activity of the new guerrillero. The anxious imitation of the selfless saint (ragged clothes, peasant food, self-abnegation, mortification of the flesh) gives way to the relief of direct action, side by side with the young campesinos he had worked with so tirelessly—and with, as he felt, so few apparent results—when he was only a parish priest. The poems to his fellow guerrilleros have several different modes: to one he says, you will suffer but you will also be transformed into something wonderful, as Christ was; to another he says, you died, but no one understands the meaning of your death; but we must die if we want to go to heaven; we'll get our "green gold," our reward, there. He speaks to his compañeros in terms of their noble mission: we'll free the skinny dogs and tie up the fat dogs. He pictures one guerrillero fleeing the Guardia: the forest opens up to let him in; the natural world is the ally of the revolutionary. And he also tells us why he himself become a guerrillero: because all the legal means of procuring justice for the poor were useless, fruitless, unworkable.

But with this shift away from self-torturing turmoil toward the joys of action, the poems also reflect the premonition of his almost certain imminent death, which worries and saddens him even as he accepts its necessity. It is not bad luck to die, he says, if you believe in the new life that death makes possible. But there's also anxiety surrounding the preview of his death: he panics, feeling death like something stabbing his windpipe; he is grieved to think he will die before he sees the Triumph; he is afraid his compañeros will mourn him, bury him, remember him in the wrong way, and he threatens to rise from the grave to punish them if they do. A touch of the old impotent rage returns when he imagines that somehow his work for the people will be changed or destroyed by nameless others, hypocrites who will pretend to weep at his funeral. And yet his greatest anxiety seems to be that his compañeros will die without him: "I want to die with them!" This is not a brief suicidal impulse; it's a sign of comradeship and solidarity.

But tracing the thematic evolution of Gaspar's poems does not tell the entire story. There is also what we might call a rhetorical shift, a change of tropes. In a sense, almost all of Gaspar's poems have some political meaning, if we take the "political" in the widest sense to mean deciding how people are to live in an unjust world. Sometimes Gaspar made unadorned political statements, as in short poems like the following:

Sin la muerte de los pobres	There never were dictators
nunca habría dictadores	nor princes, nor bosses
ni príncipes, ni señores,	nor oppressive tyrants
ni tiranos opresores.	who could do without the death
	of the poor.

Or:

Tu país es mi país,	Your country is my country,
marginado,	outcast,
tu ranchito, mi casa;	and your farmhouse, my house;
es tu escasez mi acicate,	your deprivation is my spur,
tu liberación, mi causa.	your liberation, my cause.

And there is the poem dedicated to the FSLN in which images of flowers seem imposed from without, decorations to what is essentially self-congratulatory sloganeering. Or there are simple, prosaic, moralistic aphorisms, such as: "The pain of others / goes by us / without sinking in."

This is pretty blunt stuff, but Gaspar also has a series of increasingly subtle allegorical modes at his disposal. By allegory I mean the presentation of a dramatic situation in which real or imaginary characters and what they say suggest meanings that transcend the immediate visual and verbal situation, like a dream we interpret even as we are dreaming it. In the simplest mode, the political meaning of the allegories is spelled out. Peace sails into the harbor and announces to the weeping people (and the weeping poet) that Peace and War are sisters. The poet compares water on the plains and water in the mountains to men who "water ideals" and those who cultivate hatreds and passions. Seeds and ideologies both need time to dry and mature before they can be useful. He wishes an oxcart would bring his ideas to the campesino, but that the ideas were the campesino's, just like the harvests. The campesino is seen plagued by an "immense lake of fathomless oppression," caught between volcanoes, "your greatness fenced in by powerful oppressors." The waves of the lake recite a lesson that the poet feels obliged to translate directly for his readers: "'Revolution. Revolution.'" But allegories that are spelled out tend to become mechanical and predictable; when they are political, they tend to degenerate into cant, cliché, and propaganda.

There is a second level of Gaspar's allegory, however, which is more subtle. He and his friends are actors in a complex drama, the meaning of which is suggested rather than elucidated. He feels himself to be "good manure / scattered in all its filth / over barren fields." The fallen guerrillero will be "crushed like wheat, / made flour for Christ, / for the world." The men of the future as the poet sees it will be "like geraniums / with strong scent / and red petals" and the women "like prolific / poppies." Gaspar's figurative language here seems looser, richer, freer than in the earlier modes. He trusts us as readers to respond to the suggestive-

133

ness of the imagery; he feels no need to spoon-feed us meaning or do our thinking for us.

And yet the mode that is most intriguing is what we might call open-ended or symbolic allegory. Here the meaning of the dramatic moments and the actors caught up in them may or may not be political. But that is less important than the almost mystical, ecstatic, oceanic quality of mind some of these poems evoke. In one, the poet is a "hotbed of poppies," a "plow to untilled lands / deep river." Or he is "inexorable tide, / violent volcano, / living flame." Or "We are / one sea with another near the shore, / foam mixed with foam, / wave with wave." Or the speaker is the flood tide itself: people on the shore watch his strength, then shake off their laziness and set forth on the force of his current and he carries them away to some new experience. Or the poet is a mat of ivy spreading through the world; or unspecified boats have been lost at sea and he wants to follow them; or his soul sails out "into a thousand perfumes" and his spiritual desert is flooded "with fragrance and well being."

I believe most of these poems were written during the last year of his life, which is to say his year in combat. How can we explain the powerful, ever-shifting, protean energy of the imagery and the joyful, self-confident fullness-of-soul these poems bespeak? I will hazard a guess, which is that in 1978, despite certain nagging anxieties, Gaspar had found himself, had found a mode of active loving and rebellious thought that, after years of frustration and dead-ends in San Juan and Tola, released his best energies, and gave his restless nature free reign and an ample field of play. The giddy, electric freedom of some of these "open-ended allegories" signals a breakthrough not simply in poetic technique, but in self-fulfillment. As he says in his 1978 letter to Silverio, he is at peace with himself and happy; if he had the choice to make again, it would be the same; he's being true to his mission as a priest; he knows the cause is just; he feels the congregation to which he belongs respects the course of action he's chosen. In short, he is at the height of his powers as his death approaches, and the poetry mirrors this.

· · · 11

But analyzing Gaspar's psychological quirks, or the religious or political history that helped shape his identity, or his poetic themes and techniques, suggestive as each approach might be in isolation, may still bring us no closer to the guerrillero, priest, counselor, friend, and example he was to so many Nicaraguans. True, he had a personal, subjective life; but he also touched the lives of hundreds of people who knew him or knew about him. True, he came out of the flow of history; but he was also *in* history and helped create history around him. For the most part his poetry was a private affair and he was always reluctant to show people what he had written; and yet he wanted the poems preserved, had some of them typed by Madelina Flores, and spoke of entering them in a competition in Spain to raise money for San Juan. And so it is to Nicaraguans and their experiences since 1970, and *their* sense of who Gaspar was and why he mattered that we need to return. He gave them his all; let them be his final judges.

Padre Frutos Valle and Padre Donald both worked with Gaspar on the Rural Outreach Teams and later, CEPA.
Padre Frutos Valle:
"What stood out most about Gaspar was his sense of friendship, carried as far as it would go. His behavior was all honesty and sincerity. He got along equally well with priests, campesinos, and city folks. When he arrived at a meeting, he filled it with life. . . .

135

"He never even remotely thought of abandoning his priesthood. And if he joined the revolution, it was because of the commitment to his people he had assumed as their priest. It was his temperament that led him to armed struggle. . . .

"'Murderer Priest'? That's what they called him when he made public that he'd wanted to kill Somoza. Oh, they had fun with that. But I think that whatever he decided would hasten the liberation of Nicaragua he would have done. . . . Not everyone who kills is a murderer; in this case it was to defend the weak. You don't just choose evil; you choose the lesser of two evils. Is that so wrong, morally? If someone can't defend himself, you've got to help him so he can do so. . . . You don't choose evil because it's evil; you choose it to keep the tyrant from continuing to do even more evil. . . .

"Gaspar loved the people so much that he gave them the best thing he had: his life."

Padre Donald:

"I knew Gaspar thanks to CEPA. But I saw him seldom. All the same, I would define him as a person of contrasts: friendly in his way of doing things, but physically brusque. His vocabulary was typically Nicaraguan; he loved certain expressions—and you know how foul-mouthed we Nicaraguans are! His way of thinking wasn't really Spanish. He thought and acted as though he'd been born and bred right here in our country.

"For us, what always set him apart was his passionate love for the campesinos. And when he reacted violently, we knew beforehand that it was because of the ill-treatment the campesinos had received. I think this was his principal motive for entering the guerrilla: to seek solutions to the problems of the campesino, solutions that would never come from the Somoza regime. . . .

"Gaspar felt himself to be something of a prophet in Nicaragua: an instrument chosen to bring about salvation. A little bit like Judith: to cut off the heads of dictators. Maybe that's why he made his attempt against Somoza. . . .

"Here's an interesting side of his life: his enormous appreciation for the beauty of creation, an appreciation which led to an enormous respect for people, for their dignity, since 'they're all children of God.' He was a poet of life. . . .

"Before entering the guerrilla he came to CEPA and asked our advice. Three times. The majority said they thought he could do a lot more from his post as pastor, preparing his people and raising their consciousness, than he could bearing arms. Martín Mateo was among those who urged most strongly that he remain. But Gaspar got angry and accused them of being cowards, of looking for excuses. Of course at that moment he hadn't made his decision yet. It was historical circumstances, the persecution of which he was the object, and the necessity of fleeing Nicaragua that pushed him toward his final decision.

"For him, the conflict was never ideological. He only sought justice. To try to confine him within the boundaries of some social movement or other would be a terrible mistake. His way of thinking was far above such things. If he went over to the Frente, it was because he saw that the Frente Sandinista, more than any other group, stood for what the people needed: justice."

Luis Enrique Mejía Godoy:
"I've always called him 'the Guerrillero Priest.' Because for me, he was. A guerrillero of peace. His example—as a man, as a Christian, as a revolutionary—always inspired sufficient confidence to convince people of good will that there was a place for them in the struggle. . . .

"Gaspar had decided to mount the bucking bronco of history. He was an authentic guide, what we call in Nicaragua a 'tayacán.' With him I came face to face with the New Christianity. So don't call me an atheist."

At the end of his prodigious labor of collecting information for *Gaspar Vive*, Padre Manuel Rodríguez asked his fellow priests all over southwestern Nicaragua to administer a questionnaire to a random sample of their parishioners, everyday folks, ordinary Nicaraguans. Let us sample a few of their answers.

1. Who was Padre Gaspar García Laviana?
"A 20th-century prophet. He announced the Good News and denounced injustice. He made the people of Nicaragua see the dignity that belongs to us as children of God."

"A person of conscience who helped us fight to get free of the slavery we were in. He was a liberator."

"A person who was very generous toward the campesinos."

"The first priest who ever made himself a campesino and fought for the human and spiritual dignity of the campesinos."

2. *What do you think of his work as a priest?*

"In San Juan and Tola he left traces that will never be erased. He taught the people to think of a God who was more human, more loving, more understanding."

"His best work was the unity he brought to the campesinos. He did a lot of good deeds. He never had any money. He always gave it away."

"He taught us what brotherhood was."

"I remember him whenever I see old folks, children, the sick, whoever's needy. He was one of us. His work was love, and he got that work done."

3. *Why do you think he entered the guerrilla?*

"To fight for our liberation."

"To get us out of the terrible situation we were in."

"Because praying wasn't enough. He had to act. And he did."

"He went to the guerrilla and died because he didn't want there to be slaves. And that's what we were. He wanted to free us from that."

4. *What do campesinos and workers think of Padre Gaspar?*

"What do you suppose somebody thinks who's learned everything he knows from Gaspar?"

"It was a shame we didn't listen to everything he said. If we had, the Nicaraguan campesino would be something very different today."

"His advice was to work. And to love each other like brothers. What can you think except good about somebody who acted that way?"

5. *Does anything remain in your town that Padre Gaspar did?*

"The Medical Dispensary."

"Everything. He did it all."

"The Casa Comunal."

"Everything. We didn't used to have anything."

"The School and the Health Center."

"The School."

"Everything."

6. *Do you think that the work of Padre Gaspar changed the campesino mentality in your town or village?*

"Yes. The campesino now thinks and feels he's a person, and not what he felt like he was before—a machine who was supposed to work to make a profit for the boss."

"He taught us how to organize ourselves, and to work united for the entire community."

"He showed us what it means to be a person. Before, we were like rusted in place, like we'd been changed into just . . . things."

7. *How do the campesinos try to put into practice what Padre Gaspar taught them?*

"Trying to do better every day, like Padre Gaspar wanted."

"Working together. We no longer have individualist campesinos, only members of a community who work in unity."

"Reading more carefully—now that we can read—the word of God."

"We didn't really understand him until he had left us. I guess the same thing happened to the Apostles with Christ."

"He was my brother. I learned everything from him and I imitate him in everything."

8. *What teachings of Padre Gaspar do you intend to put into practice in your life?*

"Help the ignorant. Teach them."

"Pray, pray, and pray."

"Follow the path the Padre laid down for us. Without fear of anybody or anything. You have to be a fighter, like he was."

9. *What concrete ideas do you remember from Padre Gaspar's thoughts?*

"He said you have to give your life for the people. Like Christ did. And he gave his. That's his best teaching."

"The way he got right to the point. For every problem he looked for a solution. Makes no sense just stamping your foot. You've got to find solutions."

"We liked to hear him talk about God—he made God's presence alive for us, brought Him down from the clouds where we'd always kept Him. Every time he spoke about the Father, it was like a wonderful discovery."

10. *How did you react when Padre Gaspar joined the guerrilla?*

"Seemed natural. I saw it as logical. He said it was alright if I didn't follow him."

"I felt sad. But then happy and hopeful. He wouldn't let us down. He'd gone to fight against injustice. And he'd come back victorious. Only, I was wrong. He didn't come back. But he did leave a foundation of justice to build on."

"I was glad. The Padre was fighting for the people, like he always said he would."

"I was amazed. I'd never thought of the Padre as a guerrillero. If he went to the mountains, he did it for me."

"I was surprised. I never thought he'd join up. All I can say is, if *he* did it, it couldn't be bad. And if he killed, he did it to save us from the oppression we were stuck in. He was defending the children of God."

"I knew he was going to die. He always went all out, right to the end, with everything. I was really upset. I was upset because I couldn't go with him. I was only 12 at the time."

"He went to join the campesinos. He'd be among his people, even though the location might have changed."

"He gave a Christian feel to the revolution."

"He lived the faith he professed. Sandinismo has a lot to thank him for. He made it something praiseworthy for all Nicaraguans."

"With him, Christ entered the revolution. The proof is in the many young people who joined the fight with rosaries around their necks. And Gaspar was always there when they needed him."

Final testimony belongs to another campesino, this time not from the San Juan-Tola region, but from Solentiname, the chain of islands in the Big Lake. Felipe Peña, as mentioned earlier, was one of the campesino poets who took part in the October 1977 assault on the Guardia garrison at San Carlos. For almost a year he languished (when he was not being tortured) in a cell in La Bartolina prison, only to be released in August 1978 when "Operación Chanchera" at the National Palace won the release of Felipe and other political prisoners. After Panama, he made his way back to Costa Rica, met briefly with his poetry mentor, Mayra Jiménez, and other poets, and then returned to combat. He was with Gaspar during the September incursion and retreat on the Southern Front. Felipe died in combat only a few months after Gaspar, only a few months before the Triumph.

A GOOD LEADER

I met you at the beginning of September
in a column of 35 soldiers of the Army of the People.
You were doing rearguard with Compañera Marta and me.
Your alias was "Martín."
You and El Danto commanded the column
and he, an expert in trekking through the mountains of Nicaragua,

was point man, leading the march.
We'd been resting in the shade of a leafy tree
we'd come across while climbing one of the hills.
We were about to move on when El Danto shouted to me:
"Hide! The planes'll see you!"
His voice surprised me
I tried to run but fell.

Another group of compañeros had made a hit on the command post
at Peñas Blancas that morning
and the air force was bombing.
We heard the rockets exploding
400 meters away.
The order came to advance.
I was all tangled up in a canebrake.
We came out into a clearing,
the brush hid us knee-deep,
and the planes went right overhead.
Angrily I shouted: "This is criminal!
They drag us out of the woods into a clearing!"
And you, Martín, shouted: "Take it easy!
When the plane comes by just drop where you are and don't move!"
Running, then freezing, we made it to a ravine.
There you took off your shoes and seeing how worried we were
said with absolute calm:
"If they drop a bomb we'll come back here;
but nobody's going to run."
We stayed there until four in the afternoon. At six
we approached a house you ordered us to take.
I got scared and timidly asked
"We're not going to . . . do anything to these people, are we?"
And you answered firmly: "NO."
You bought a pig and two chickens from them.
The night was rainy,
we lay down in shacks where hens were roosting.
Compañero Malicia was shaking with fever
and there were no blankets.
And the following night we came back,
having given up any chance of attacking the Rivas command post.

On the main road a [Costa Rican] guardsman arrested you,
and deported you to Panama,
but later I saw you again in camp
directing drill from five to six in the morning
and in the evening holding political discussions.

And I remember that because of you
they didn't send me to another camp.
After that I lost track of you
until I heard the news
that the Guardia of the tyrant had killed you in a firefight,
and heard you named "the priest Gaspar García Laviana."
Back when I knew you I didn't know you were a priest;
for me you were just a good leader,
devoted body and soul to the people's struggle.

Every year since 1978, on December 11, at exactly 5:06 a.m., the people
of San Juan perform the following tribute to Gaspar: every pistol, shotgun,
rifle, anti-aircraft gun, and firecracker in town is shot off at once. For a
minute or so the earth shakes. Every bird in town bolts into flight, banking this way, then that, to avoid the noise echoing off the huge rocky head-
lands to north and south. Then the last shot, and the town falls silent
again. Slowly, the birds settle back into the trees. Then the sun rises.

Appendix

A GASPAR GARCIA LAVIANA

Un buen día nos llegó
a tiempo completo Gaspar
de Asturias el Misionero
que araba sobre la mar.

¡Su voz por Tola se oyó,
por Rivas Gaspar pasó,
y Angel, Martín y Miguel
cayeron los 3 con él!

Logró cambiar la parroquia,
sotana y confesionario
por montaña y Evangelio,
fusil revolucionario.

Estalló la madrugada
Malinche, granada en flor,
y al final de la jornada
era más brillante el sol.

TO GASPAR GARCIA
LAVIANA

One fine day when the time was
    ripe,
Gaspar came to us,
the missionary from Asturias
who plowed and threw seeds on
    the sea.

His voice was heard in Tola,
through Rivas his footsteps took
    him:
"Angel," "Martín," and "Miguel,"
all three of them fell with him!

He ended up changing his parish,
cassock and confessional
for mountain, Gospel,
and revolutionary rifle.

Dawn exploded like
a cluster of Malinche blossoms,
and at the end of the day
the sun shone more brightly.

143

¡Su voz por Tola se oyó,
por Rivas Gaspar pasó,
y Angel, Martín y Miguel
cayeron los 3 con él!

Sabía que llegaría
la muerte sin avisar,
pero la muerte es semilla
cuando hay un pueblo detrás.

"¡Agarra bien la guitarra,
jodido!" decía Gaspar.
¡Su corazón guerrillero
nunca dejó de cantar!

¡Su voz por Tola se oyó,
por Rivas Gaspar pasó,
y Angel, Martín y Miguel
cayeron los 3 con él!

His voice was heard in Tola,
through Rivas his footsteps took
   him:
"Angel," "Martín," and "Miguel,"
all three of them fell with him!

He knew death
would come without warning,
but death is a seed
when the people stand behind
   you.

"You jerk! Hold tight to that
   guitar!"
said Gaspar.
His guerrillero's heart
never stopped singing!

His voice was heard in Tola,
through Rivas his footsteps took
   him:
"Angel," "Martín," and "Miguel,"
all three of them fell with him!

—Luis Enrique Mejía Godoy
Costa Rica, diciembre 1978

["Angel," "Martín" and "Miguel" were three of the aliases used by Gaspar after his decision to take up arms against Somoza. When the singer Luis Enrique Mejía Godoy wanted to join up and fight, Gaspar told him: "Listen, you jerk! You hold onto that guitar and sing. That's your best weapon."]